"Greg Coles has become one of the most important voices in the church. I can't express how grateful I am for him and for this book. *No Longer Strangers* is another home run—showing us a creative, bold, and intrepid way forward in following Jesus in a gray world. I commend him to you. And his melodic book."

A. J. Swoboda, author of *After Doubt*, assistant professor of Bible and theology at Bushnell University, Eugene, Oregon

"Equal parts delightful and sobering, Greg Coles relates his experience of being a third-culture kid to the alienness of the Christian life. Self-deprecating without victimizing himself for all the ways he's felt different or out of place, he levels the ground for all of us who have always felt a little extra or a lot not enough. Come for the stories, and leave with a bit more hope for the future church and all the different ways Christ draws us in and sends us out."

Lore Ferguson Wilbert, author of *Handle with Care: How Jesus Redeems the Power of Touch in Life and Ministry*

"When I finished reading *No Longer Strangers* I thought that all of my friends should read this book, because in its pages they will find a friend in Greg, hope for the church, and true belonging with Friend and Lover, Jesus Christ."

Laurie Krieg, podcaster, teacher, and coauthor of *An Impossible Marriage: What Our Mixed-Orientation Marriage Has Taught Us About Love and the Gospel*

"Greg's book is most 'delightful,' to use one of his often-used expressions. I enjoyed reading about his quest for belonging through various friendships, among his peers, families, with his God, or his church community. His skills in adjusting to his environment, a third-culture-kid characteristic, is key in his crossing various cultural bridges. Like most TCKs, Greg is a gem of a friend. His writings reveal his pursuit of being authentic and vulnerable while honoring his Indonesian roots, celibate gay Christian core, and wonderful sense of humor. What a delightful book!"

Lois J. Bushong, licensed marriage and family therapist and author of *Belonging Everywhere and Nowhere*

"Simply superb. Theologically excellent. Deeply personal. Brutally honest. Intensely engaging. Coles's writing is simply exquisite. He moves from vivid description of personal experience to profound theological reflection with the ease of an exceptionally gifted writer. A must-read."

Ron Sider, distinguished professor emeritus of theology, holistic ministry, and public policy, Palmer Seminary at Eastern University, author of *Rich Christians in an Age of Hunger*

"Structured around compelling narrative, *No Longer Strangers* is a story of the human quest for acceptance and belonging. Greg Coles, in his winsome and honest way, takes all of us on a journey to discover the places, the people, and the God in whom and to whom we all belong."

Deb Hirsch, missional leader and author of *Redeeming Sex: Naked Conversations About Sexuality and Spirituality*

"Greg Coles is one of the most talented Christian writers I know. His writing is remarkably vivid, whimsical, and poignant all at the same time. I believe that God has raised up Greg Coles as a unique voice to speak with excellence and grace to a number of challenges that the church faces today. I want to read everything he writes!"

Michelle T. Sanchez, executive minister of Make and Deepen Disciples, Evangelical Covenant Church

"I have a group of writers I call my 'print pastors'—people who help to shepherd me along the Christian way through their books. Greg Coles is in that group. His insightful meditations on the Bible, lively stories, humble and humorous self-disclosures, and timely invitations to a more faithful, missional life are some of the things God has used to convict and comfort me. Read this book slowly and reflectively, and let Greg pastor you too."

Wesley Hill, associate professor of New Testament at Trinity School for Ministry, Ambridge, Pennsylvania, and author of *Washed and Waiting*

"In *No Longer Strangers*, Gregory Coles offers a heartfelt and compelling exploration of what it means to belong to Jesus and to others, especially when we feel the ache of being an outsider. With engaging storytelling and incisive theological reflection, Coles invites us into the journey of finding our home, not only in Christ but in the beloved community where aliens become brothers and sisters."

Sharon Garlough Brown, author of the Sensible Shoes series and *Shades of Light*

"In his new book *No Longer Strangers*, Greg Coles explores belonging in a deeply personal panorama of his life. It's a book about real connection. The engaging stories are layered through multiple aspects of his crosscultural and mobile life, creating a very Christian, very human experience. Read it."

Michael V. Pollock, author of *Third Culture Kids: Growing Up Among Worlds*

"In this profound book, Greg Coles revisits a familiar but essential theme of the Christian life—being an alien pilgrim. The exploration he takes the reader on echoes voices of the past like Paul or Augustine of Hippo, only with the added vibrancy and poignancy of his experience as a celibate gay Christian. Sharing a similar journey myself, this book wonderfully captures what it's like to be totally alien in a culture and church that has compromised by making its home here. This is a riveting and deeply personal memoir of living in the now-but-not-yet tension of being a disciple of Christ in a world that doesn't always understand the search to live for the greater good of God's presence. Coles provides a rare and rich opportunity to gain insight into the reality of following Christ in the ultimacy of its beauty, difficulty, and hope. This book is for those who refuse to compromise and instead live for the deeper joy of finding their 'haven sweet of rest' in Jesus Christ."

David Bennett, author of *A War of Loves: The Unexpected Story of a Gay Activist Discovering Jesus*

"Greg Coles has done it again! He's managed to produce a book that is just as beautiful as it is meaningful. With wit and charm, Greg invites you into his journey of belonging—a journey you never want to end. Greg helps us see that the twists and turns in our own journeys are what make them significant. This book is a real page-turner!"

Preston Sprinkle, president of The Center for Faith, Sexuality & Gender

No Longer Strangers

Finding Belonging in a
World of Alienation

GREGORY COLES

Foreword by JEN POLLOCK MICHEL

An imprint of InterVarsity Press
Downers Grove, Illinois

InterVarsity Press
P.O. Box 1400, Downers Grove, IL 60515-1426
ivpress.com
email@ivpress.com

*InterVarsity Press® is the book-publishing division of InterVarsity Christian Fellowship/USA®, a
movement of students and faculty active on campus at hundreds of universities, colleges, and schools
of nursing in the United States of America, and a member movement of the International Fellowship
of Evangelical Students. For information about local and regional activities, visit intervarsity.org.*

*While any stories in this book are true, some names and identifying information may have been
changed to protect the privacy of individuals.*

*This book is published in association with Nappaland Literary Agency, an independent agency
dedicated to publishing works that are: Authentic. Relevant. Eternal. Visit us on the web at
www.NappalandLiterary.com.*

Cover design and image composite: David Fassett
Interior design: Daniel van Loon

ISBN 978-0-8308-4790-7 (print)
ISBN 978-0-8308-4791-4 (digital)

Printed in the United States of America ∞

*InterVarsity Press is committed to ecological stewardship and to the conservation of natural resources
in all our operations. This book was printed using sustainably sourced paper.*

Library of Congress Cataloging-in-Publication Data
A catalog record for this book is available from the Library of Congress.

P 25 24 23 22 21 20 19 18 17 16 15 14 13 12 11 10 9 8 7 6 5 4 3 2 1

Y   37 36 35 34 33 32 31 30 29 28 27 26 25 24 23 22 21

For Zack Filbert,

superb alien company

on this foreign Planet Earth.

Contents

Part Three: Belonging To

Foreword

Jen Pollock Michel

I finished this wonderful book in the cramped front seat of my minivan. My sixteen-year-old daughter and I had arrived early (or so we thought) to the DMV on a Friday morning at the end of summer. As we turned left into the parking lot, we groaned at the snaking line, more than seventy-five people deep. We parked and took our place at the back of the parking lot. "How long do you think we should expect to wait?" the couple in front of us asked the DMV employee with the bullhorn. (It was his job to remind the bedraggled crowd that due to pandemic protocols, only customers with birthdays between January and June would be served.) "From here? Probably two and a half hours." I was glad to have jammed my laptop into my bag before leaving, just in case.

To begin here—in the front seat of my minivan, on the all-important driver's license errand for my sixteen-year-old daughter—is to give a glimpse into the differences between Greg Coles and me. As a gay, celibate man, Greg leads, for the sake of his commitment to Jesus, a "childless, sexless life." As the married mother of five children, I find myself on a Friday morning at the DMV, writing this foreword and practicing road test questions. On the surface, Greg and I might seem to share little in common beyond our Christian faith and our writerly vocation. In many churches, divided by demographics, Greg and I would remain practical strangers, finding ourselves in different small groups, different Sunday school classes, different pews, and at different Sunday lunch tables.

The voices of cultural common sense (and sadly, some churches) insist that belonging should be construed according to homogeneity. In this version of the good news, we belong to one another by virtue of our shared socioeconomics, our shared educational levels, our shared politics, our shared racial and ethnic identities, our shared domestic situations. Belonging is determined fundamentally by likeness. But this is tenuous belonging at best. The kind of belonging that's forged by sameness will be the kind to both exclude as well as include, to exile as well as welcome. Circles of sameness, especially in a fractured age like ours, seem inevitably positioned to constrict rather than expand.

But as Greg Coles so convincingly argues in this book, the gospel's version of belonging is far stranger, far more wonderful, and far more resilient than any insiders' club. The wide-armed promises of belonging in the Christian faith center on Jesus, who bore exclusion on the cross in order to tear down every dividing wall between humanity and God—and between every "us" and "them."

Like Greg, I've spent most of my life suffering the chronic feeling of estrangement. As a child, I constantly moved from place to place, never staying long enough to put down anything resembling roots. As a young adult, I faced the premature deaths of my father and brother, which forced me to reckon early with this world's cruel impermanence. Now ten years into the immigrant experience, I'm still struggling to answer the most elemental questions about home. Is home the place you leave? The place where you receive mail? For human beings, belonging is one of our most visceral desires. We long to be received, to be taken in. We want to be recognized and, in our absence, missed. These are the longings that I've known in my own story of mobility and grief—and also the longings that Greg has known in the airports of his childhood and in his "alien" calling of celibacy. We both know something about the inhospitality of this world and the elusiveness of earthly belonging.

But this is also to say we know something about hope.

There are many reasons why I might commend Greg's book to you, but it seems no small thing to suggest that readers will find it immensely hopeful. I don't mean hope as religious cant. Greg's hope for belonging is found in the gospel, yes, and as otherworldly as it is, it's also marvelously entangled in the affairs of everyday life. Greg's hope is present as he folds laundry with friends, as he teaches impossibly long words to a pair of elementary-aged brothers at his church, as he shows up to hourly wage jobs and unwittingly makes friends. Greg's hope isn't removed from the suffering of the world. It's present in the awfulness of goodbyes, in the heartbreak of consequential disagreement, in the tensions of what we can only dimly understand this side of the veil. Greg's hope both weeps and reassures that tears will one day be dried. In other words, this isn't a book that traffics in warm and fuzzy pieties. It's a book that is storied and human, narrated by one man who is braving the cold winds of this world and avowing the warm arms of Christ. This is a book whose writer assures every reader: wherever you come from, whatever baggage you carry, you can belong too.

When *No Longer Strangers* had only just begun to take shape, Greg tried to explain his vision for these pages to Jane Crandell, his white-haired friend at church. She took his hands in hers, veined and weathered by years, and told him belonging mattered, that it might be the best invitation we could offer to this homesick world of ours. Jane knew, as Greg knows, that belonging is not just the balm of Gilead to salve our own wounded souls. It's something we offer to other wounded pilgrims, who wonder where to find shelter, who can't begin to imagine an expectant father at the end of their very long road, who must be encouraged to smell the feast.

Whether you feel at home in the world or you don't, the belonging that Jesus offers to each of us is good, sure news. It is good, sure news for us—and also for the world.

Tentacles

An Introduction

When we were kids, my best friend Zack claimed 1 Peter 2:11 as his favorite Bible verse. He would scrunch the freckled skin around his eyes, as if searching for the words in midair, and recite in boyish singsong: "Dear friends, I urge you, as aliens and strangers in the world, to abstain from sinful desires, which war against your soul."

Or at least, that was what he tried to say. In reality, he only ever got this far: "Dear friends, I urge you, as aliens . . ."

At the word *aliens,* he would lose his composure and collapse into a fit of helpless giggles. It never failed. When you're in elementary school, aliens are always hilarious. Aliens in the Bible? Even better.

Unfortunately for today's Christian youngsters, the updated 2011 version of the NIV doesn't use the word *aliens* anymore. Now it reads, "Dear friends, I urge you, as foreigners and exiles," which is probably more precise but nowhere near as much fun. Fortunately for Zack and me, we grew up in a simpler time, when "tweeting" was for birds instead of presidents, and 1 Peter was indisputably full of aliens.

Twenty years later, it's still impossible for me to read 1 Peter 2:11 without hearing it in Zack's voice. I pause right after the word *aliens,* leaving time for two eight-year-old boys to laugh so hard they spray spit at each other. And then I let Zack finish reciting the verse to me, explaining in his boyish singsong why these aliens are out of place, how they're called to follow Jesus on this foreign Planet Earth.

I try to picture the aliens as I assume Zack pictured them: people from every tribe and tongue and nation who love Jesus, and who also happened to be tentacled extraterrestrial beings covered in slime. I picture green-gray skin and hairless, bulbous skulls and UFOs emblazoned with the Beatitudes. I picture people who will never quite feel like they belong, because the world they live in wasn't made for people with tentacles.

I picture Zack's tentacles. I picture my own.

In my mind's eye, I let myself become an alien.

○ ○ ○

Belonging has never come easy to me. Growing up, there was my mutated national identity to deal with—my not-quite-American, not-quite-Indonesian soul, restless in both countries. There was my lack of skill in soccer and video games, those hallmarks of boyhood success. There was my awkward body, first pudgy, then gawky, always remarkably white for an Asian. There was my insufferable eggheadedness, the kind of isolation known only to an eight-year-old who reads *Hamlet* and then memorizes the famous soliloquy ("To be, or not to be . . .") just to show off.

In middle school, I read a book about a really smart kid who starts slurring his words to blend in with his peers. I tried it, and became for a brief season the middle school boy with both a Shakespearean vocabulary *and* a stoner's articulation. People were kind, but this did not improve my popularity.

I was good at belonging in church, where mild-mannered and musically inclined boys are highly prized. I ran the PowerPoint slides and played violin and had insightful things to say during

Bible studies. Church ladies always wanted to set me up with their daughters and granddaughters. But I was never interested in their daughters and granddaughters, because I was busy trying very hard *not* to be interested in their sons and grandsons.

Two decades later, when I finally came out as a celibate gay Christian, the secondhand marriage proposals ended abruptly. Suddenly, I wasn't quite so good at belonging in church anymore.

These days, as I watch my close friends pair off in marriage and start having children, I wonder what it means to belong with other people if I never build a family of my own. As I scramble to figure out what city or state or country I'll be living in next year, I wonder what it means to belong in places I can't stay in forever. As I realize what an oddity I am in so many of my groups—an oddity among Christians, an oddity among LGBTQ people, an oddity among academics, an oddity among Americans—I wonder what it means to belong to others even when I can't manage to blend in with them.

I used to believe that my placelessness made me a rarity. I assumed that most people fit naturally into their environments, found the tribe they were meant to join, and never had any doubt about where they belonged in the world. Everyone else had been told the secret to feeling claimed and understood, the secret to fitting somewhere. I alone had missed that day of second grade (because I was homeschooled, probably), and I was doomed to be a misfit for the rest of my life.

But the longer I live—the more I study people and get to know them—the more I believe we're all still learning how to belong.

According to Abraham Maslow, humans are predisposed to chase after five basic sets of human needs. Belonging is halfway up Maslow's hierarchy, sandwiched between safety and esteem—right at the heart of the pyramid we spend our whole lives trying to climb. We fight to fit somewhere, even when everything around us is transient. We form tribes out of our ephemeral identities—the gluten-free tribe, the young mothers' tribe, the kayaking enthusiasts' tribe—because we long to be among people who will act like us, people who will think like us, people who will *like* us, even if just for a season.

We settle down at "permanent addresses" that might be abandoned for a larger model, a smaller model, another neighborhood, another city. We build friendships that time or distance or a difference of opinion could unravel. We root ourselves in a world with an expiration date.

○ ○ ○

"Foxes have dens and birds have nests," Jesus tells a prospective disciple in Luke 9, "but the Son of Man has no place to lay his head."

I wonder whether this would-be disciple ended up following Jesus after such a disheartening recruitment speech. Luke doesn't tell us one way or the other. Frankly, the prospects seem grim. Why give up everything for a leader whose signature promise is that you'll be permanently out of place?

Then again, when Peter makes this very complaint to Jesus, Jesus responds by promising his disciples two lifetimes' worth of belonging: "No one who has left home or brothers or sisters or mother or father or children or fields for me and the gospel will fail to receive a hundred times as much in this present age: homes, brothers, sisters, mothers, children and fields—along with persecutions—and in the age to come eternal life" (Mark 10:29-30).

The way Jesus tells it, if we give up on belonging in order to follow him, we'll find ourselves belonging anyway, as if by accident, in spite of ourselves. We might not belong the way other people do, with normal homes and normal families and normal ways of fitting in. But we'll belong in a way that's a hundred times better, fully in place because we know we are out of place. We'll belong in all the weirdest ways, finding family among strangers, making homes out of tents that are better than mansions. We'll belong like aliens.

We human beings have a habit of doubting Jesus when he makes wild promises like this. I don't think Jesus minds our doubt. In fact, I think he loves showing off to us over and over again how faithful he is. I think he loves making us gasp in wonder as our lives turn up new pieces of evidence that he meant what he said.

Maybe you're caught in the same tension as me, wanting to fit somewhere even as you're permanently out of place. Maybe you're not quite sure how to belong. Maybe you feel like an alien.

If so, come journey with me. Learn to belong alongside me. Gasp in wonder with me.

Let's be aliens together.

PART ONE

Belonging In

Maybe your country is only a place you make up in your own mind. Something you dream about and sing about. Maybe it's not a place on the map at all.

HUGO HAMILTON

Womb Nostalgia

Notes from an Alien Anthropologist:
Once grown, the human creatures seem to believe their place in the world can be earned. It is only their youngest offspring who truly understand the species' helplessness.

I get nostalgic when I think about my life as a fetus.

To be clear, I don't remember much from those days. Whatever mental notes I took back then never made it into long-term storage. Still, I like to imagine that I did a lot of deep thinking with my tennis ball–sized fetal brain, philosophizing into my amniotic fluid. If I'd been a twin, and we'd had some sort of telepathic connection, my twin would have been like, *Woah. This guy's deep.*

The way I imagine it, being in the womb is like soaking in a perfectly warm bath. My eyes are closed, everything shrouded in gentle blackness. The sounds I hear are also sounds I feel: the pulsing of two hearts—one close by, one distant—and the murmur of voices that reach me in vibrations through the water. One of these voices is richer than all the others, more all-consuming. It is the voice of my mother—the voice of the universe herself.

All I need is the atmosphere I call home. I'm immersed in protection, immersed in nutrition, immersed in oxygen, without needing to claim anything for myself. Each moment and its gifts come to me unasked for, undeserved. Tastes and smells are automatically included with the rental package. It never occurs to me to earn something. There's nothing to try harder at, nothing to get anxious about. I'm not on the way to anywhere.

I exist.

That's all.

That's enough.

○ ○ ○

I paid my mother's womb the highest available compliment by delaying my birth until a full week after my due date. My older brother John, by contrast, had arrived two weeks early, his exploratory impulse manifesting from the very start. *(What happens if I swim down here?)* But I was an incurious and cozy child, perfectly content to stay put. I was in no rush to go out adventuring and wreck a good thing at home.

My mother, unfortunately, did not take my tardiness as a compliment. She went on a lot of long walks, eager to evict me. As for my siblings, they mimicked Mom's eagerness. All three of them, in preparation for my arrival, had learned the words to a children's song that began, "Welcome to the family / We're glad that you have come / To share your life with us." They were excited about me, even though I'd done nothing to earn their excitement. They had decided I would belong. It was never a question in their minds: *Will the infant be worthy of love?* They loved me before I'd done anything lovable.

Laura, the five-year-old, was hopeful that I would turn out to be a little sister. Since my parents weren't the sort to find out the baby's sex in utero, Laura enjoyed seven months or so of wishful thinking before I foiled her plans by coming out with male parts and getting named Gregory Joshua instead of Amy Margaret. She took the news in stride and began honing her diaper-changing and weightlifting skills on me.

My brother John's very first memory as a two-year-old is of peeking over the top of my parents' quilted bed, just after my mom and I returned home from the hospital, and gazing transfixed at the sight of the little brother he'd been waiting for. When I started crying, as is the custom of newborns, John instinctively took the posture of the protective older brother: "Mom, he's sad! Can't you help him?"

Strange, isn't it, how my life could begin in a world that cared far more about me than I cared about it?

I saw a video once on *America's Funniest Home Videos* of a little boy tapping his mother's pregnant belly and asking, "Do you have my brother in there, Mama? Do you have my brother in there?" When she answers in the affirmative, his mouth widens and he breathes in deeply, as if hearing this news for the first time. "Oh, thank you, Mama!" he shouts, wrapping his arms as far around the belly as they can reach.

My life as a fetus was the life of that little brother. I was embraced before I could feel it, before I knew what it meant to be embraced.

Perhaps our best moments of belonging are always the moments we can't earn.

○ ○ ○

I grew up around the phrase "born-again Christian." It felt normal to me, the same way it felt normal that my oldest brother, Jeff, started teaching me SAT vocabulary words when I was six years old, the same way haggis probably feels normal to Scottish people. "Born again" was the term we used to differentiate people who *really* loved Jesus from the ones who just attended church as a matter of ritual. I never spent much time thinking about the weirdness of the concept. I pitied Nicodemus in John 3 with a patronizing kind of pity. *Silly Nicodemus, to misunderstand something so intuitively obvious.*

Sometimes our words become so familiar that we forget what they mean.

But when I stop to think about it, I sympathize with the consternation Nicodemus feels when he learns that entrance into the kingdom of heaven requires a second birth: "How can someone be born when they are old? . . . Surely they cannot enter a second time into their mother's womb to be born!" (John 3:4). Nicodemus is picturing fully grown people trying to clamber back into wombs, trying to reattach umbilical cords to their bellybuttons and take another soak in the amniotic sac.

Weird.

And Jesus' reply doesn't exactly clear up the confusion: "Very truly I tell you, no one can enter the kingdom of God unless they are born of water and the Spirit. Flesh gives birth to flesh, but the Spirit gives birth to spirit. You should not be surprised at my saying, 'You must be born again'" (vv. 5-7).

Still weird.

Next time someone tells you they don't think "born again" is a weird way to talk about the Christian life, ask them how they envision "the amniotic sac of the Holy Spirit." See if that gets a rise out of them.

For Nicodemus, a Pharisee of religious and political standing, spirituality has always been a matter of learning and earning the things of God. His first words to Jesus in John 3 are, "Rabbi, we know . . ." (v. 2). God's presence is a cognitive matter. Nicodemus has seen the kingdom of God, he believes, because his religious training has prepared him to see it.

Jesus' reply—"No one can see the kingdom of God unless they are born again" (v. 3)—is nothing less than a rebuke of Nicodemus's self-confidence. Whatever Nicodemus can see of the kingdom of God isn't something merited by his extensive learning. It can only be a gift, given as Nicodemus is birthed from the womb of the Holy Spirit, helpless as a fetus, sustained by the grace of his Creator.

The return to the fetal state makes us uncomfortable. It runs contrary to everything we've learned in our tit-for-tat, pull-yourself-up-by-your-bootstraps world. We're predisposed to believe that, in order to belong somewhere, we have to earn it. That to be welcomed by anyone—and by God most of all—requires our most intense efforts. That being helpless inevitably leads to being outcast.

But the uncomfortable claim of Jesus is just the opposite: that the only way to God is the way of the fetus, the way that does nothing more than helplessly exist within the atmosphere of God's grace. To know Jesus is to approach him in weakness. Faith can't be conjured up by trying harder at our religious labors. Participation in the kingdom of God begins the same way my life as a fetus began: with a series of unearned and undeserved gifts.

○ ○ ○

I've heard people say that our passage from this life to the next one will be like a baby's passage through the birth canal. We'll leave behind the tiny womb that has been our universe and emerge into something grander than our wildest imaginations. All the vocabulary of our old lives will be insufficient to scratch the surface of our new lives.

I'm partial to the way this analogy expands our conception of what heaven might be like. (With the caveat that, frankly, I'm hoping our early months in heaven involve a wider variety of beverages and a lot less feces than our early months on earth.) But what I love most about the picture of heaven-as-birth is what it teaches us about our present moment. If passing into heaven is like being born, then our lives on earth are as incomplete and temporary as our months in the womb.

We still know the universe in such a limited way. We still think the limited thoughts of someone philosophizing into amniotic fluid. We still hear God's voice with underdeveloped ears, like vibrations passing through the water.

Now we see like unborn children, imagining with our eyes closed. Then we shall see face to face.

Early on an April morning in 1990, after subjecting my mother to a thirty-six-hour labor, I left the womb and stared for the first time into the face of the woman who had been my entire universe. I had tried to delay that first birthday, hanging onto the womb for every extra second I could get. But my belonging in the womb was never meant to be permanent. It was belonging-with-an-expiration-date, belonging in a home that could only carry me until the time came to find a new home.

One of these days, I'll die and pass into a new kind of life. I'll look again into the face of the One who has been my protection, my nutrition, my oxygen. Maybe, when that next birthday comes, I won't be so afraid to say goodbye.

Leaving the womb, after all, is just the beginning of the story.

Home Sweet Airport

Notes from an Alien Anthropologist:
On airplanes and in airports, the human creatures finally escape their arbitrary and restrictive national borders. Strangely, very few of them seem to relish this experience.

I spent the better part of my toddler-hood roving the contiguous United States in a brown van. My family lived off peanut butter sandwiches, chomping apples down to their ragged cores as we stared out at an eternity of cornfields. We slept on the living room floors of strangers my parents had known in college. Time passed in increments of bathroom stops.

If you're thinking this lifestyle makes us sound like hippies, you're not entirely wrong. In the 1970s, my parents were part of the bohemian-evangelical crowd called the Jesus Movement. Dad had long curly hair and preached from the steps of the student union wearing a wooden cross around his neck. Mom bought whole wheat flour in bulk and made a lot of granola. By the 1980s they were homeschooling their children, back in an era when most homeschoolers were either joining a cult or stocking their basements for a nuclear apocalypse.

With a family like that, there was no question I would turn out to be weird, at least by most American standards. The only question was *how* weird.

My parents answered that question definitively when they decided to move to Indonesia.

The handwriting had been on the wall since 1987, three years before I was born, when my father first dreamed of taking our family to Africa. He pitched the idea to my mother, who at the time was pregnant with my older brother John, and she promptly burst into tears. For months, he kept on pitching, and she kept on crying. The Africa plan died a long, lachrymal death.

But shortly after my birth, the Indonesia plan emerged, rising like a phoenix from the ashes of the first plan. Both parents—even my adventure-averse mother—felt a clear sense of calling from God this time. We set off in our brown van to get trained, raise support, and prepare for the adventure of a lifetime.

Perhaps the rest of the family felt uprooted, being dragged around the country and then flown across the globe after so many halcyon years in upstate New York. But I had no reason to feel uprooted. My toddler feet had never stood still long enough to take root in the first place.

In true homeschooling fashion, our road trip across the United States was peppered with "educational field trips": detours to Niagara Falls and Carlsbad Caverns and Great Sand Dunes National Park. No doubt my three older siblings learned a lot by visiting these landmarks. But I wasn't exactly the right age to be savoring aesthetic and intellectual grandeur. To this day, I can ask my mom something like, "Have I ever climbed the Statue of Liberty?" and she'll answer, "Yes, but you were nineteen months old and we had to carry you most of the way up."

Youth, they say, is wasted on the young.

One of our homeschooling field trips—long since forgotten by me, but preserved in Coles family lore—took us to a Wild West historical park. After a full day of reading educational plaques and watching gunslinger showdown reenactments and missing my nap,

I wanted to go home. With dramatic two-year-old wails and inflections, I announced to my parents: "I want my vanny-van!"

The rest of the family seemed to think this was funny. I probably laughed too, because when you're the youngest of four siblings, you do a lot of laughing at jokes you don't understand. As far as my thesaurus was concerned, *home* and *van* were perfectly valid synonyms.

I didn't know enough to feel entitled to a home without an odometer.

O O O

My childhood's significant milestones all occurred at three-year intervals. (My mom also has a master's degree in math. Coincidence? I think not.)

My siblings and I were each born three years apart, like clockwork: 1981, 1984, 1987, 1990. In 1993, three years after I was born, we moved to Bandung, the third-largest city in Indonesia. We furloughed back to the United States every third summer—1996, 1999, 2002, 2005, 2008—and beginning with Furlough Number Two, we left behind whichever older sibling had just graduated from high school and was ready to start college.

When we moved to Indonesia, the season of the vanny-van technically came to an end. Neither our temporary first house in Bandung (borrowed from my parents' coworkers for six months while we got our bearings) nor our more permanent second house was fitted with wheels. Neither seemed in any danger of changing locations.

Still, I never totally escaped that toddler feeling that my home was in motion, transient, always on the way to somewhere new.

Once I was old enough to count by threes, I was perpetually counting down to my next life-altering voyage. Another series of plane rides around the globe. Five months of itinerant American existence. Another sibling casualty to higher education. More plane rides. Two-and-a-half years in the country I knew best, even though my family members kept deserting it one by one—and even though, someday, I was supposed to leave it as well.

Indonesia and the United States seemed to belong in two different universes. Air smelled different, buildings looked different, food tasted different, people acted different. Cars were built in mirror images of each other and drove on opposite sides of the road. Different animals participated in daily life: where the United States had domesticated pets, Indonesia had neighborhood-browsing chickens and tiny lizards called *cicak*, which crawled along our house's concrete walls eating mosquitoes.

It was as if each country had been invented by a fantasy author living in the other country. Everything was similar but fundamentally altered, a zany storybook reinvention of itself. All the colors were reassigned. All the horses turned into unicorns.

Case in point: milk. Our Indonesian milk came in flimsy one-liter plastic bags delivered on the back of a motorcycle. The milk was unhomogenized, its pale cream clinging to the bags as we emptied them into a pitcher. We saved the cream, one tiny trickle at a time, in a plastic Tupperware container in the freezer, until we'd stored up enough to churn in the blender and make a precious lump of butter. (Real dairy butter was exorbitantly expensive, so we mostly used tubs of MeadowLea brand margarine. *Cholesterol-free*, the tub proudly announced. My best friend Zack and I, delighted by the rhyme, wouldn't simply ask people to please pass the butter; instead we said, "I have a plea for the MeadowLea cholesterol-free.")

When our fresh milk ran out or soured, or when the delivery motorcycle broke down, or when we traveled to places without good refrigeration, Indonesia had other milk options. We would beat milk powder and water into a beige froth, or we'd buy ultra-high temperature (UHT) milk, which came in waxy boxes and could last for months at room temperature.

Whether fresh or powdered or boxed, we called all these drinks "milk." But none of them tasted much like the American beverage, purchased in plastic jugs at grocery stores. American milk boasted of its cream content with percentile names and yet somehow had no streaks of cream floating on its surface. It was delicious, but almost too delicious, like one of those absurdly good-looking and talented people you want to hate because they are insufficiently flawed.

When I drank Indonesian milk, the thought of American milk felt fictional. When I drank American milk, Indonesian milk became something from a dream. My world was defined by the nation I lived in at any given moment. The other nation—its sights and smells and patterns of life—felt as distant as a fairy tale.

○ ○ ○

Airplanes and airports were the portals between my universes. They were the in-between thing, neither fully American nor fully Indonesian, and I loved them for that. Unlike every other nonhuman feature of my life, air travel was the same in every country. I returned to it again and again, familiarity increasing my fondness, celebrating its landmarks like a treasured vacation destination: *Ah, beloved ticketing counters, where we weigh our checked bags and repack at the last minute to avoid overweight costs! Ah, joyous security lines, an endless flow of testy strangers getting partially undressed together! Ah, overpriced duty-free shops and overcrowded boarding gates and overworked flight attendants with kerchiefs around their necks welcoming us aboard! Ah, carry-on luggage jammed in overhead compartments, seats too close together, lavatories with frighteningly loud toilets, tray tables in their upright and locked position!*

"Airports are so homey," I told my parents when I was in high school. We were in the Jakarta airport at the time—not an airport that inspired gladness in the average traveler.

My parents gave each other meaningful looks that said, *What have we done to this child? Is the damage permanent? Do we have enough in savings to cover his future counseling fees?*

The truth was, knowing that all my fellow travelers felt displaced put me at ease. Perhaps my delight was partly schadenfreude, but I suspect it ran far deeper. In all my other homes, someone else had more right to call the place "home" than I did. Indonesia belonged to its citizens first and foremost, it seemed, and to me only in a partial and secondary way. As for the United States, I was barely more than a glorified tourist, no matter what my birth certificate said.

But in airports, for once, I belonged just as much as everyone else. I could be a misfit in airports, because airports are entirely populated by misfits, and when everyone is out of place, everyone belongs.

For once, I could be exactly the same as the people around me. No one was staying. We were all just passing through.

O O O

Before deciding to go to Indonesia, my dad hadn't gone to a doctor for a physical exam in years. He was still in his early thirties, in the prime of health, and he didn't see any reason to go wasting money on hospitals. But the move overseas forced him into a doctor's office for a reluctant quinquennial check-up.

That was the only reason his doctor found the melanoma.

Years later, when my dad was swimming or when our games of family wrestling got sweaty enough to merit going shirtless, I would see the deep red scar along his back, the pit of flesh a surgeon had carved out to keep the cancer from spreading. It was a visual reminder of how easily the story might have had a different ending—how easily stage II might have become stage III, stage III might have become stage IV, stage IV might have become a somber ceremony and a pile of earth and a fading memory.

"Do you ever wish that you had a more normal childhood?" friends have sometimes asked me. "Do you ever resent your parents for dragging you along on their quest to follow God, all the challenges you didn't get to choose, that persistent childhood feeling of homelessness that made you fall in love with airports?

Wasn't it unfair that your life had to be hard because of your parents' choices?"

When I try to imagine the other life I could have had—the theoretically easier life, the life where airports don't feel so homey—I also have to imagine a life where my father wasn't forced into a doctor's office. A life where no one might have seen the melanoma until it was too late, until the cancer had already metastasized. A life where my father might have been dead before I learned how to speak his name.

My parents had the power to spare me the challenge of life overseas. But they didn't. Instead, they followed God, and God in his kindness spared me from so much more.

The promise of Christianity is not that God will endorse whatever path we determine is best for ourselves, whatever path seems most likely to result in our own happiness and the happiness of those we love. The promise of Christianity is that God calls us to a path better than all the best things we thought we wanted. In pursuit of Jesus, everything must be lost so that everything can be found. Everything must be made homeless so that everything can finally be made to belong.

○ ○ ○

In the Hebrews 11 "Hall of Faith," the first evidence given for Abraham's radical faith is his radical itinerancy:

> By faith Abraham, when called to go to a place he would later receive as his inheritance, obeyed and went, even though he did not know where he was going. By faith he made his home in the promised land like a stranger in a foreign country; he lived in tents, as did Isaac and Jacob, who were heirs with him of the same promise. For he was looking forward to the city with foundations, whose architect and builder is God. (vv. 8-10)

Abraham's testimony is the kind that doesn't get much airtime in evangelical churches today. There's no tidy ending to the story of his homelessness. He journeys into the unknown and never emerges in a country that feels like his own. He spends his whole life in the middle, a stranger on the way to somewhere. By faith, he makes his home in airplanes and airports.

I can almost hear present-day pastors and elders declining Old Abe's offer to speak at their churches. They ward him off with firm handshakes and pats on the shoulder: *It sounds like your story isn't quite ready to be shared yet. You just need to wait on God a little longer. Once you get fully settled in the promised land, we'd love to hear that testimony of God's faithfulness.*

But Abraham's faith is exemplary precisely because he's still a stranger at the end of the story. Even the land he's buried on has to be bought specifically for that purpose, because no piece of the promised land belongs to him. His faith is a foreigner's faith, an unsexy faith, a faith that's terrible for boosting attendance or tithing numbers. Instead of taking him all the way home, Abraham's faith takes him only as far as the *promise* of home. And this, apparently, is the point of the story:

> All these people were still living by faith when they died. They did not receive the things promised; they only saw them and welcomed them from a distance, admitting that they were foreigners and strangers on earth. . . . They were longing for a better country—a heavenly one. Therefore God is not ashamed to be called their God, for he has prepared a city for them. (vv. 13, 16)

If Abraham hadn't still been longing for something at the end of the story, he wouldn't have been living by faith anymore. The longing, the waiting, the uncertainties and tents and promises—these were the things that marked him as an alien. And God, whose kingdom has no immigration bans and no extradition treaties, is eager to make homeless aliens into citizens.

○ ○ ○

There comes a time in every young man's life when he grows out of being a Handsome Little Guy and blossoms into a prospective domestic terrorist.

I was nineteen when it happened. My passport was expiring, and I needed a new photo to mail in with my renewal application. The drugstore attendant operating the camera forbade me from smiling—not because the passport office had a rule against all smiling, I later learned, but because this particular drugstore attendant disliked happiness. My eyes, stripped of their glasses, widened and unfocused and glazed over like a junkie's. When the camera shutter snapped and my picture appeared on the screen, it could have been an ad campaign for juvenile delinquency awareness.

I probably should have asked for a retake, but that would have cost extra. And as a sophomore in college, I was nothing if not frugal.

That same year—who can say why?—airport security started taking much more interest in me.

Before then I had been just a Handsome Little Guy with an oversized backpack, trailing dutifully behind his parents and sporting all the malicious intent of a cheese curd. Now I was an adult, a potential threat, a scraggly-faced lowlife with the passport photo of an axe murderer.

During those college years, I was "selected at random" a disproportionate number of times for additional screening. I certainly wasn't being profiled in the way my friends of Middle Eastern descent sometimes were in the days after 9/11, when airport security turned overnight from a cordial game into a fearful ritual. But even the modicum of suspicion I encountered as a grungy hoodie-wearing white man cast a shadow over my old sunny memories. Some part of the magic of airports, the homey charm I fondly remembered, began to dwindle as I left childhood behind.

Homes come and go, even when those homes are airports.

I do a lot of air travel these days, and I still love it. I'm that guy who shamelessly pulls out his toothbrush in the men's bathroom of the Detroit airport, freshening up at the sink while a stream of hurried strangers passes by. Mostly I get a lot of strange looks, but one time, a guy pulled out his own toothbrush and asked to use some of my toothpaste.

"You're making yourself right at home," he said, accepting the tube I held out for him. "I admire that."

I spat into the sink. "I hear that home is wherever you keep your toothbrush. Even if you're just passing through."

He laughed and wished me a safe trip to wherever I was going. I wished him the same.

I didn't tell him how long my journey was going to be. I didn't tell him that my whole world sometimes felt like an airport—like I was only ever passing through, living in tents, subsisting on promises of a future I couldn't see. I just packed up my toothbrush, hoisted my home onto my back, and stepped out into an adventure big enough to last a lifetime.

3

Poohsticks in an Open Sewer

Notes from an Alien Anthropologist:
The human creatures often wish for unusual things to be made ordinary. If their wish is granted, they end up losing the very things they cherish most.

The upstairs toilet of my childhood house in Indonesia emptied, through a series of pipes, into an open sewer flowing along the north edge of the house. If I happened to be out on the porch when someone else was flushing the toilet, I could look down the slender concrete gap that separated our house from the house next door to see a liter of waste water splash out of the pipe's open mouth and into the sewer. Or, if I flushed the toilet after attending to my own business and then ran down the hallway fast enough, I might make it onto the porch in time to witness the waterworks.

Maybe you call this gross. I called it cool. Potato, po-tah-to.

Some of the Western adults living in my city, Bandung, talked about our open sewer system like it was a bad thing. They preferred more discrete forms of sewage disposal (something about germs and public health). I had no such preference. To my mind, hiding the sewers away made streets boring. Our plumbing-in-plain-sight was a source of entertainment. An urban waterfall-on-demand.

In the evenings before bed, my dad used to read aloud to us kids from A. A. Milne's Winnie-the-Pooh books. Even though we were the ones lying in bed, he was always the one falling asleep, his eyelids drooping as he read slower and slooowwweeerrrr and slllloooooooowwwwwwweeeeeerrrrr until we yelled, "Wake up, Dad!!!!"

He would jolt upright, choking back the beginning of a snore. "Just resting my eyes!" he would protest, and then carry on reading.

The Winnie-the-Pooh stories were full of ideas I adopted as my own. To describe the pre-lunch hunger that plagues those who eat an early breakfast, I found there was no better label than Pooh's phrase "feeling a little eleven-o'clock-ish." The snack to satisfy such hunger was "a little smackerel of something." And when no snack was available, no expression of consternation could top Eeyore's glum "oh, bother."

My brother John and I also found a promising pastime in the game Poohsticks, in which Pooh Bear and his friends would each find a stick in the Hundred Acre Wood, drop their sticks into the river at the same time, and see whose stick made it to the other side of the bridge first.

The street outside our house in Bandung had no rivers, but it did have open sewers. Practically the same thing.

Thus was born our own urban Indonesian reimagining of Poohsticks. Instead of combing the forest for sticks, John and I would comb the streets for pieces of trash. We raced our trash against each other in the sewers, watching it navigate past obstacles made of protruding rock and bits of discarded metal and literal sticks of poo. Far more exciting than a plain, obstacle-free river.

The sewer that formed the racetrack for our games ran underground twice, passing once beneath our driveway and once beneath the street before reemerging at the gate of our local middle school. The underground segments of the track heightened the suspense of each race. Sometimes our trash would get caught in there and never reemerge. Sometimes it would drift out ten minutes later, long after we'd given up on it, dislodged by a new piece of trash from our latest race.

The art of the game was all in selecting the perfect piece of trash. Candy wrappers floated well, but they were so light that they easily got trapped in the hazards of the racetrack. Cigarette butts had fewer jagged edges that could be snagged on a stray piece of wire, but sometimes they got waterlogged and sank into the roiling brown river. Broken bits of wood or hard plastic were rarer finds, and they could spell near-certain victory if they didn't sink or mysteriously disappear in the stretches of underground.

When friends came over to play with us, Poohsticks was a crowd favorite. Everyone else also had open sewers and trash in the streets by their houses, but our sewer network had the most consistent waterflow, and our streets had a wide trash selection. How could we not celebrate these distinctive features?

○ ○ ○

Our Bandung house was full of "distinctive features." Some of these features—like the rooftop view of the surrounding mountains—were universally celebrated. Others, like our open sewers and our extensive trash selection, weren't exactly the sort of features that look good on a real estate brochure.

We had sharp red tile stairs with no railing, and low ceilings above the staircase (four feet, eleven inches at the lowest point) where my brother Jeff taped yellow clearance signs. Despite the posted warnings, some guest or family member occasionally failed to duck, and those ceilings claimed more than a few IQ points. I grew so accustomed to ducking as I climbed staircases that, when I moved to the United States, it took me years to stop randomly ducking on other people's stairs.

At the top of the staircase, there was an unexplained concrete lump that created a dust-filled, impossible-to-reach nook in the corner. An uncooked popcorn kernel fell into the nook once, and since we couldn't retrieve it, it sprouted months later into a corn plant right there in the upstairs hall.

Because the house had been built in multiple stages, there was an obvious seam running through the upstairs hall. The floor was disjointed, so that one side of the hallway was raised eighteen inches above the other. A gutter that had once run along the outside roof now ran through the middle of the upstairs ceiling. During a few rainstorms, the gutter clogged with leaves and sent sheets of rainwater flooding into the hall, where we collected as much water as we could in buckets, sopped up the rest with towels, and took pictures of the indoor waterfall.

To the outside observer, these household traits might have looked like defects. They were unusual, and sometimes inconvenient. For me, though, there could be no wishing them away. The austere tile stairs were perfect for tumbling Slinkys, watching them take wide drunken steps from one landing to another. The eighteen-inch rise in the upstairs hallway became the central architectural feature of countless building-block projects undertaken with John. The lump at the top of the staircase and the ceilings with clearance signs meant the staircase was *my* staircase and not someone else's.

If I had wished them away, home wouldn't have been home anymore.

○ ○ ○

If you're anything like me, you've spent a shocking amount of your life wishing that its atypical features could be made more typical. You've bemoaned your shower faucet with the cold and hot water lines switched, the one you always forget to explain to houseguests (which is why your houseguests keep accidentally freezing or scalding themselves until they figure it out). You've complained about your weird neighbors, the ones who blast the radio at 11:00 p.m. while sitting on a front porch apparently decorated for a low-budget horror film. You've longed at times for someone else's simpler childhood, a single town or state or country to belong to.

You've stared at your face in mirror after mirror, mentally photo-shopping out each mole and scar and asymmetry until you look like someone more perfect than you.

You've dreamed of a life copied from a Pinterest photo, a life so smooth and spotless it has no more stories to tell.

In Japanese art, there is an aesthetic ideal called *wabi-sabi*. Beauty in *wabi-sabi* has nothing to do with perfection or uniformity. On the contrary, the imperfections in a piece of art make it unique and particular. Uniqueness and particularity make it beautiful. Cracks, blemishes, asymmetries: the things I'm always trying to get rid of are the celebrated necessities of *wabi-sabi*.

It's human nature, I think—it's certainly *my* nature, at any rate—to try to iron all the wrinkles out of life. When we feel like we don't belong, we try to solve the problem by making things a little more uniform, a little more ordinary. We take what we've been told are the best bits of other people's lives and set them as the preconditions for our own satisfaction. We search for home by enforcing someone else's vision of what the word *home* means.

Along the way, we overlook the quirky beauty within the wrinkles, the beauty that has always belonged to us and only us.

If we want to find our place in the world, we have to let our lives be particular, personal, idiosyncratic. We have to live like we're fearfully and wonderfully made, like we're God's *wabi-sabi* works of art. How could we possibly belong on someone else's terms when we weren't made to fit in any other body, any other story but our own?

o o o

It's been years since I've played Poohsticks in an open sewer. (Central Pennsylvania, for all its admirable qualities, offers tragically few Poohsticks courses as exciting as the one from my childhood.) But to this day, when I hike past an idyllic creek or stream or river running through the woods, I sometimes find myself comparing it to the ugly, beloved sewer running past my childhood home.

There's no sense asking which is better, which I would rather be standing beside. Trying to answer that question changes nothing and benefits no one. I'm certainly not wishing that the rocks and sticks and foliage of my current home will be transmogrified into the rusted metal and feces and plastic bags of my youth. But neither do I wish that the rusted metal and feces and plastic bags of my youth had been exchanged for a sewage-free Pennsylvanian paradise.

I'm grateful for what was. I'm grateful for what is. I'm grateful that I chose—that I still choose—to belong to them both.

Maybe someday I'll learn to love my own quirks and blemishes as much as I loved those childhood games of Poohsticks.

Standing on the bank of an idyllic creek or stream or river, I sometimes kneel to the forest floor and pick up a wizened leaf or a bit of bark. Silently I count to three, drop it in the water, and watch as it catches the current. My eyes follow its progress until, finally, it drifts out of sight.

4

The Man Who Coughed
Blood on Me

Notes from an Alien Anthropologist:
Seen from the outside, the differences between human beings appear insignificant. Through their small eyes, however, the human creatures perceive enormous differences between themselves.

Because I was homeschooled, I'm allowed to make fun of homeschoolers. I don't make the rules. I just reap the rewards.

"Have you seen the Homeschool High-Five?" I'll ask a group of people whenever the subject comes up. As they profess their curiosity, I make a great show of emptying my hands, stretching my shoulders, flexing my fingers, as if I'm preparing for a gymnastics routine of Olympic proportions. And then, once I have everyone's attention, I raise both hands and slap them together.

Occasionally someone doesn't get the joke, and I'm forced to exposit: "Because we have no friends. We have to high-five ourselves."

In defense of my homeschooling tribe, I ought to tell you that the jibe is false on two counts. First of all, even though homeschoolers don't have "school friends" in the traditional sense, most of us have siblings at home being schooled alongside us, available for high-fives in moments of enthusiastic need. Second of all, homeschoolers can and sometimes do have plenty of friends outside of school. If anything, being homeschooled gives us more

homework-free time and more scheduling flexibility to accom-
modate our social calendars.

Admittedly, some of us may be socially awkward, present
company included. But I dare you to find a public school (let
alone a private school) that isn't also largely populated by
awkward people. Those who live in pubescent houses shouldn't
throw stones.

Still, like all good comedy, the Homeschool High-Five has
some nuggets of truth to it. I first remember feeling it in second
grade, when my parents sent me to the local international school
in Bandung to take a series of standardized aptitude tests with the
other second graders. For three days, I spent every recess beneath
the patchy shade of a banana tree, squinting at the properly ma-
triculated kids as they swung across the monkey bars. They might
have included me in their games, if I had asked, but asking never
occurred to me. I just assumed I was the sort of person who had
no place with them. I was adept at self-imposed isolation.

In third grade, I joined the soccer team at that same international school, where I spent the next four years publicly demon-
strating my athletic incompetence. (At the end of the sixth-grade
season, my coaches awarded me "Most Improved Player," which I
took to mean, *You may still be a gubbins on the field, Coles, but you've
tried very, very hard.*) I barely spoke to most of my teammates,
because I assumed they had cooler, more athletic school friends
already and weren't in the market for poorly coordinated homeschool acquaintances. I didn't even attend the sixth-grade soccer
awards ceremony, because no one remembered to tell me it was
happening. Instead, a coach turned up on my doorstep the following afternoon to offer me a laminated "Most Improved Player"
certificate and a stern-faced handshake.

Sixth grade was also the beginning of youth group, yet another
social sphere populated by kids from the international school.
There were a few other homeschoolers there, as there had been on

the soccer team and in the second-grade testing room, and we banded together in nerdy solidarity. But in the mystical calculus of middle school popularity, I was confident that I still belonged in a low social stratum. If there had been a banana tree available, I probably would have stood underneath it.

People like to joke that homeschooling eliminates the need or opportunity for social interaction. In my case, it did nothing of the sort. I was in physical proximity with my "real-schooled" peers often enough, speaking at least one of the same languages, sharing at least a handful of the same interests. And yet, through no fault except my own, I remained convinced that I belonged in a different silo of humanity than they did.

Homeschooling wasn't the only thing isolating me from the crowd. There was money to consider as well. By Indonesian standards, I grew up outlandishly wealthy. I lived in a house with sit-down toilets, enjoyed a ready supply of food, and had access to the best medical care Indonesia could offer. I had traveled farther as a first grader than most Indonesians would be able to afford in their entire lives. I embodied my neighbors' definition of luxury.

Despite all this, I rarely *felt* wealthy. I felt like a normal person who just happened to be surrounded by poor people. Wealth is like greener grass, irritating habits, or unwavering self-assurance: it's one of those things only *other* people can have.

To be Caucasian in Indonesia was to publicly advertise my wealth everywhere I went. As far as the average Indonesian street-goer was concerned, I might as well have worn a T-shirt sewn from one-hundred-dollar bills. Young men would fall in step beside me as I walked through the streets, introduce themselves, spin a quick tale of their financial woes, and ask me for money before we'd gone three blocks. As soon as I became passably adolescent, young women flirted with me regularly—not because I was "dreamy" by any objective standard (possessing as I did roughly the same suaveness and skin quality as a horned toad), but because they were gold diggers and I had the coloring of a gold mine. A kid of about eight once gave me a friendly high-five, told me his name, asked for mine, and then demanded that I buy him a pizza.

In the people group we lived among, the Sundanese, saying no was considered rude. "*Maaf*," I would say instead, as I continued walking. "I'm sorry." Sometimes it was hard to tell what I was apologizing for: their poverty, or my riches?

Hardest of all to face were the vocational beggars. The ones who still had two legs tended to wait at street corners, especially young children leading their blind grandmothers from car window to car window when the traffic light was red. Other beggars hunched along the busiest sidewalks, nursing severed stumps as flies buzzed lazily around them. They looked up at me with vacant eyes as I walked past, seeing the obvious wealth in my face, daring me to see their obvious poverty.

Sometimes, if I'd brought spare change with me, I would stop and place a paper bill worth fourteen cents into their outstretched hands or the clay bowl at their feet. "God bless you," the bolder ones would say, or bow to touch their forehead to my hand in thanks. Sometimes I didn't have change, and the bolder ones would yell after me, calling me names that don't translate politely into English. But the beggars I remember best were the ones who never spoke at all, only stared—stared at me like they knew I belonged in a different silo of humanity than they did.

In the unofficial caste system of Indonesian life, I was a Brahmin, elevated, immaculate, nearly godlike. They were Untouchables, the lowest of the low. None of us had asked for our place in the hierarchy, but none of us expended much effort trying to overturn it. It seemed inborn, immutable, a birthmark no amount of scrubbing could erase.

Whenever I had no small bills to give, I would let my eyes drift past the beggars without stopping, without acknowledging their presence, as if they were nothing more than protrusions in the concrete. I told myself it was to spare their feelings, to keep them from getting their hopes up in vain. More likely, ignoring them spared my aching conscience from the burden of compassion. I was rehearsing the fine art of being physically proximate to others, speaking at least one of the same languages, sharing so much common humanity, and yet remaining worlds apart.

How hard it is for the rich to enter the kingdom of God.

○ ○ ○

My parents' policy on school attendance was that we kids were welcome to choose whether we preferred to be homeschooled or international-schooled, as long as we took responsibility for our own transportation to school in the latter case. I took the leap in ninth grade, enrolling in just one or two classes a year at first, then becoming a full-time student at the international school in twelfth grade. Almost every weekday for four years, twice a day, I commuted the forty minutes to school by foot and by *angkot*, a network of shared vans that served as the public transportation of choice for working-class Indonesians. ("You ride *angkots?*" a horrified classmate at the international school asked me. "Isn't that dangerous?" To which I replied, "Not so far.")

My commute began with a kilometer-long walk. First, down the short narrow hill of my street, past smiling neighbors sitting in the meager shade of their front steps, past an Independence Day mural that depicted a uniformed Dutch colonizer with a gun being stabbed through the stomach by a shirtless Indonesian with a bamboo pole.

At the bottom of the hill, the road came to a T and I turned left. On my right, I passed a roadside stand that sold iced young coconut milk sweetened with condensed milk. On my left, a store that sold pirated movies, then was shut down by the police, then reopened only to be shut down a second time. Farther down the road, spanning both sides of the street, a large mosque and *pesantren*—a Muslim religious school—that was home to the famed TV preacher Aa Gym.

At the next major intersection after the mosque, I crossed a busy street and boarded my first *angkot*: a flat-fronted, Dodge A100–style van. Most *angkots* were painted green, with a colored stripe just above the wheels to indicate their route. A single accordion door on the left side was tied permanently open, where passengers ducked inside to sit along two long benches running the length of the van. Once the benches were full, one or two people—always men, usually men under forty—would hang out the doorway, right legs planted on the boarding step, right shoulders lodged against the ceiling. My brother John and I loved nothing better than to ride hanging out of the *angkot* doors; we were quick to chivalrously offer up our seats to women and children when things got crowded.

Crowded, like *wealthy,* was a relative term in Indonesia. I had ridden elevators in the United States that were considered crowded if anyone had less than fifteen inches' personal space on all sides. Indonesian *angkots* had no such arbitrary rules. We sat jammed up against each other, thighs pressed together, shoulders overlapping. The same van might have held eight passengers if I had been riding it in New York on furlough; in Indonesia, I once rode an *angkot* carrying twenty-one adults.

My school commute required two *angkot* rides. The first took me south for ten minutes or so—either a light-blue-striped *Kalapa Ledeng* or a black-striped *Cicaheum Ledeng* would do. The second, a dark-blue-striped *Ciumbuleuit Stasiun Hall,* took me up the long, steep Ciumbuleuit Road to a quiet tree-rich neighborhood where my school campus was tucked away. (The words *cium bule* could ironically be translated to "kiss a white person," but I was told this had nothing to do with the origin of the road name.)

When I was ready to disembark each *angkot*, I would call out "*Kiri*," asking the driver to pull over to the left side of the road. Sometimes he (the driver, too, was always a man) would stop right where I hoped. Other times he wouldn't hear me, so I would clear my throat and call a second time, and then my fellow passengers would join me in shouting "*Kiri kiri!*" as we overshot my stop by fifty meters. I would squeeze past my seatmates' knees, give the driver the fourteen cents I owed for the ride, and murmur my thanks. Driver and passengers alike would study me, wondering what a rich kid was doing on poor people's transportation, taking curious sidelong glances like I was a millionaire in line at a soup kitchen.

○ ○ ○

The morning of the strangest *angkot* ride I ever had, I was wearing my favorite T-shirt—for the last time. It was soft and loose-fitting, solid gray, with stripes of blue running around the collar, along the shoulders, and down the sleeves. Logo-free, too, which made me feel mature for some reason. Graphic tees and corporate emblems were for kids. Solid colors meant you had your life together.

I boarded the second *angkot*, the *Ciumbuleuit* one, just before a handsome but haggard man who might have been in his thirties. The benches filled until we were pressed up against each other, my cargo pants against his khakis, cozy strangers. Neither of us paid much attention to the other at first, our gazes fixed forward and down at the corrugated steel under our shoes. I didn't look up until he began tapping me on the shoulder.

He seemed to want to speak, but his throat looked caught, like someone choking on a bony bite of fish. He jerked his hand toward himself repeatedly.

"*Maaf,*" I said, "*nggak mengerti.* I'm sorry, I don't understand."

His eyes widened urgently. He tried to reach past my head but failed, his range of motion limited by the bodies crowded around him. He tapped the window and jerked his hand again.

"*Ingin buka jendela?*" I asked. "You want to open the window?"

He nodded vigorously. He seemed to be swallowing something back now, as if he were about to vomit. I released the black plastic latch, superheated by the sunlight, and pushed the sliding window as far toward him as I could. He set a hand against my shoulder and tried to shove me out of his way as he began to cough and spit.

From the corner of my eye, I could see flecks of blood shooting out the window. But despite his best efforts, only a fraction of the blood he coughed up made it through the window. The rest spattered the windowsill, speckled the cheap seat cushion still imprinted with the shape of my back. And some of it, I could feel, landed on me.

He coughed for a minute or so, hacking and spitting so fiercely that I was sure his lungs must have burned. No one else in the crowded *angkot* spoke. We all looked away, pretending not to see or hear, as if we could give him privacy by becoming statues. Some people clutched their wallets, knowing a scene like this might be a scam orchestrated by a pickpocket.

When the coughing fit was over, the man sat motionless for a moment. Then he eased his hand away from my shoulder and said quietly, "*Tisu?* Tissue?"

"*Maaf,*" I said, shaking my head no.

He turned to the rest of the statues around us, a hint of pleading entering his voice. "*Tisu? Tisu?*"

A woman near the door fished one out of a plastic pouch in her handbag. He took it and dabbed around his lips, wiped off the blood on the seatback. He tried to wipe the blood from my shirt, but it had already soaked into the fabric. "*Nggak apa-apa,*" I said. "It's no problem."

He clutched the bloodied tissue for twenty or thirty seconds, his gaze returning to the corrugated steel floor. Then a second coughing fit came, less startling this time but just as fierce as the first. More blood out the window. More blood on the seatback. More blood on me.

His hand was clutching my shoulder again. I could almost imagine he was leaning on me for support, grasping for comfort from the nearest available human. But I knew he was pushing me away instead, trying to spare me the vulgarity of his sickness. It didn't matter how tightly pressed our bodies were against each other. There was a distance between us that had nothing to do with physical proximity. He didn't want his life brushing up against mine; or, at least, he was convinced I wouldn't want my life brushing up against his.

Maybe he was right. Maybe we were just two silos side by side, isolated by our very nature.

When the second coughing fit had subsided, he called *"Kiri"* in a fragile voice, and the *angkot* screeched to a stop. He gave the windowsill and seatback one last wipe-down with his crumpled tissue and left without another word.

As the *angkot* rolled away, the rest of us began to breathe again. *"Kenah TB,"* said the woman who had given him the tissue, after checking to make sure her coin purse was still full. "He has tuberculosis." The rest of us hummed in sympathetic agreement.

My stop for school came a few minutes later. I carried my backpack in front of me like an infant, not wanting to set it against the bloodied back of my T-shirt. Once on campus, I made a beeline for the nurse's office. "Definitely tuberculosis," she said. "Blood doesn't carry the infection, so you're probably fine. But after the incubation period we should give you a PPD, a skin test, just in case."

"Do you think he'll be okay?" I asked.

"There are antibiotics," she said. "I just hope he takes them. I hope he can afford them."

"I wish—" I said, and then stopped. What did I wish? That I could make sure he was okay? That I could track down one nameless stranger from among the hundreds of thousands of

Indonesians with tuberculosis, from among the tens of thousands of Indonesians who would die of tuberculosis in that year alone? That I could learn his name, pay for his antibiotics with my un-earned American wealth, and declare that his blood mattered to me as much as my own?

If I spoke it aloud, I knew it would sound like a foolish wish, an impossible wish, a child's wish.

The nurse offered me an itchy blue polo, which I pulled over my T-shirt to cover the bloodstains. "You could take off the other shirt and wear the polo by itself," she said, but I declined that offer. Too itchy, I told her, which was at least part of the reason.

When I got home that afternoon, I peeled off the T-shirt and threw it directly into the trash. I stood in the shower, scrubbing with soap far longer than necessary, at once relieved and ashamed at how easily I could rinse away all the evidence of another human being's proximity to me.

○ ○ ○

Emmanuel, Jesus is called. God with us. God in proximity to us.

If Jesus treated proximity the way I so often do, his incarnation wouldn't have been so scandalous an event. He could have made his appearance on earth with a polite degree of removal, like a benevolent monarch condescending to visit the countryside for an afternoon, like a doctor with blue nitrile gloves and a face mask stepping into the patient's room only as long as necessary. He could have placed himself in a different silo of humanity than the rest of us are in. (If anyone deserves a silo of humanity all to themselves, it's Jesus. Beyoncé might also merit such a silo, but only secondarily and for less theological reasons.)

Instead, Jesus had a habit of touching others and allowing them to touch him—even the lepers and known miscreants, the people whose physical and spiritual maladies could have repulsed him. He attended house parties not just with the tax collectors who expected to be judged by him, but also with the Pharisees who took great delight in judging him. He sought out disciples who were wildly different from him and from each other, disciples who would never have sat at the same table with one another in a high school cafeteria.

Jesus didn't abide by anyone else's silos. Young or old, rich or beggar, healthy or bleeding, holy or heinous, Brahmin or Untouchable—the boundaries all dissolved in his company. No one was left lingering under the shade of a banana tree, because neither superiority nor inferiority had the power to keep anyone isolated. Jesus descended from the highest possible place, crushing each rung of the ladder on his way down, until he was proximate to the lowest people he could find.

Emmanuel is not just the God who makes a begrudging cameo in our lives, the God who sits on the *angkot* and tolerates us for ten minutes before yelling "*Kiri!*" and excusing himself. He is the God who stays, the God who claims us as his own, the God who refuses to be shoved out of the way, even when we begin to bleed on him. He is the God who says, "Let me take all your burdens and make them mine. Let me bleed instead."

Emmanuel makes our proximity into something sacred.

○ ○ ○

I have national anthem issues the way some people have daddy issues. As a kid, I didn't understand what "ramparts" I was supposed to have been watching in "The Star-Spangled Banner." I only knew about "ram parts," which I saw whenever our Indonesian neighbors slaughtered a ram for a wedding festival or an *Idul Adha* ceremony. Why, I wondered, were the Americans watching ram parts, and why had they decided to fly a flag directly overhead? Was it a nationalistic animal sacrifice situation? Were they just hungry?

I still sang the words, but I couldn't shake the feeling that I was singing them ironically, the way I sometimes sang "O Canada! Our home and native land!" or *"Deutschland, Deutschland über alles"* just for kicks.

The Indonesian national anthem begins with the words, *"Indonesia, tanah airku, tanah tumpah darahku."* ("Indonesia, my land and water, land where my blood has been shed.") The harmonies were delicious, and so I sang them with gusto, despite my uncertainty over whether the words applied to me. Was Indonesia mine? Did skinning my knees and bleeding onto the dirt and asphalt qualify me as someone whose blood had been shed over Indonesian soil? Could I be part of this nation, belong in it, while still admitting that I didn't wear the weight of its history or own a stake in its future?

My neighborhood's Independence Day mural became a metonym for my inner life. I was both the Dutch soldier and the Indonesian patriot, both the tall white outsider and the one who had lived his formative years attached to this land and water. Maybe I was condemned to keep stabbing myself in the gut with a bamboo pole on into perpetuity.

Four days after my high school graduation, I sat in a taxiing airplane on the tarmac of the Jakarta airport. I was America-bound, just as I had been every three years for my entire life. This time, though, I didn't know when I would be coming back.

Through smudged plastic and layers of Plexiglas, I stared out at passing strips of grass and dirt. There was nothing remarkable about them; if anything, the grass looked too dehydrated, the dirt too dusty, to qualify as inviting or idyllic. And yet I found myself longing to reach through the window and touch them one last time. Longing to kick off my shoes and run barefoot through them (even though going barefoot in Indonesian soil meant I'd have to take worm medicine afterward).

Beneath the steady hum of the airplane, I began quietly singing: *Indonesia, tanah airku, tanah tumpah darahku.*

The words finally felt true. Maybe I couldn't swear to dedicate my life to the advancement of this one nation—but of course, I couldn't in good conscience swear that about the United States either. There was only one nation I was pledging total allegiance to, and it wasn't on a world map. I belonged in Indonesia as much as I belonged anywhere short of eternity. I was bound to this land and water, *my* land and water, by the simple magic of proximity, by the sacredness of our shared space.

I wanted to live it all over again, to live it so much better. I wanted to live it with no more silos in the way.

The engine noise stilled for a moment and then swelled. We hurtled down the runway, tilted back, and pulled away from the ground. I hunched over the window, watching Indonesia shrink smaller and smaller, until its streets and rice fields and mountains looked like a child's playthings. No one else could see my contorted face or the intrepid tear charting a course around the nosepiece of my glasses. For all they knew, I was just enjoying the view.

As it turns out, sometimes we belong in a place both too little and too much. Too little to stay. Too much to leave without losing a piece of ourselves in transit.

5

Hide and Seek

Notes from an Alien Anthropologist:
The human creatures seem to think conformity is the key to belonging, even though the ones most obsessed with fitting in appear least comfortable in their own skins.

Each time I reentered the United States as a kid, one of my first public acts was to go grocery shopping with my grandmother. I was always blown away by the scale of the undertaking, the seemingly endless aisles with shelves stacked to the ceiling, the wide selection of foodstuffs that I mostly knew as rare imported luxuries. Sometimes I would use the situation to my advantage. "Teddy Grahams!" I would exclaim, sincere but also conniving. "Wow, I almost forgot those existed!" And my grandmother, her usual pragmatism sabotaged by my adorableness, would deviate from her grocery list and add a box to our cart.

On one such trip, I remember whispering to Grandma as we entered the store, "It's so weird."

"What is?" she asked, bending toward me as our cart rattled forward.

I glanced around the building and lowered my voice to a whisper. "There are so many white people in here."

When I lived in Bandung, I didn't see many people who looked like me, and I already knew (or at least knew of) most of the white people I did see. On the rare occasions a white-skinned stranger appeared, I would gawk shamelessly. Once while I was riding an *angkot* with my sister, I tapped her arm excitedly and pointed out the window with my thumb. "Look," I said, using the Indonesian slang word for a white person: "a *bule!*"

Laura's eyes widened in older-sisterly mortification. "Don't point, don't point!" she whispered urgently, jerking her hand downward as if hoping to pull mine down with an invisible string. "It's rude, even when you do it with your thumb. Also, you do re-alize you're white, don't you?"

"I guess," I said. "But they're, like, white-white."

I was rife with hypocrisy. I hated being called a *bule* by others, hated being stared at for my abnormality. But when the tables were turned, I was guilty of the same fascination as everyone else.

Between the ample shelves and the ubiquity of white people, my grandmother's grocery store always felt like a sensory overload. It was like spending three years searching the night sky for a rare shooting star, only to look up one night and discover that three-quarters of the stars were suddenly shooting.

○ ○ ○

When I first got to college in New York, I avoided the topic of Indonesia with most of the people I met. I certainly wasn't ashamed; if anything, my national and cultural hybridity made me feel far more interesting, far more cosmopolitan, than I had any right to feel. But explaining my story to a stream of new acquaintances still felt unbearably burdensome. So I decided to play it cool, to see if I could pass as a "normal" American. I wanted to know what it felt like not to be marked as a minority.

During New Student Orientation, I told people I was from Potsdam, in the uppermost part of upstate New York. Since I had been born there and spent the summer before college there, this was sufficiently true. It was only when people asked follow-up questions ("What high school did you go to?" "How did you like growing up in Potsdam?") that I was forced to clarify. The rest of the time, I slid under the radar. People assumed I was one of their American-bred ranks, and I was happy to let them.

It wasn't lost on me that my campus's students of color—a relatively sparse minority at the time—didn't have the same luxury I did. Their difference advertised itself, whether they had grown up in the United States or overseas like me. They could be marked as different regardless of how much or how little they felt their race and ethnicity had shaped them, regardless of whether they were in the mood to feel different at any given moment. They were always Black, always Latino, always Asian.

As for me, all my differences from the white American majority could be hidden unless I chose to reveal them. I wore my Indonesian-ness like a New Student Orientation name tag, an optional identity, taken off and pocketed for all the moments I preferred not to be known.

And the fact that I was gay? I didn't even bother making a name tag for that. I shoved it deep into the recesses of my heart, where it could never threaten the belonging I craved.

It made perfect sense to me at the time that uniformity must be the gateway to belonging. Those who looked alike, thought alike, acted alike would be the ones who fit together. Difference was division.

Wasn't it?

One of my fellow first-year students was a guy named Kenny. Kenny sang and played piano—which I also did, though with considerably less panache—and had excellent taste in hats. To my knowledge, Kenny was one of exactly two openly gay students on our campus of about twelve hundred undergraduates. He made no attempt to blend in with anyone else. He acted fully and flamboyantly like himself.

We differed in many ways, Kenny and I. In racial identity, in life experience, in musical ability, in theological conviction. But the difference I remember feeling most aware of was the difference between my desire to fade invisibly into the crowd and his reckless, relentless willingness to stand apart from it.

For that, I both admired and feared him.

One afternoon, I was sitting in the library café with a mutual friend when Kenny approached us and began complaining about his disappointing love life. We offered our condolences. "I can help you find someone," the mutual friend said. "I just need to know what kind of guy you're looking for."

Kenny thought about it for a moment. "I want you to find me a guy who's just like Greg," he said. "Except gay."

We all laughed, because it was the obvious thing to do. "I'm both flattered and sorry to disappoint," I said. "If I find someone, I'll let you know."

Kenny, if you're reading this: I found the guy you were looking for. Alas, he's unavailable.

o o o

I often hear the accusation that celibate gay Christians talk about our sexuality too much—or, perhaps, that we insist on talking about it at all when we ought to be silent and blend in. The act of naming sexual orientation—the adoption of an identity term other than *Christian*—stands in the way of union with Christ and his followers. Or so the argument goes.

Though the circumstances certainly aren't equivalent, I hear a similar argument made about racial minority folks who want to talk about their experience as racial minorities and the ongoing challenges they face. I hear it made about survivors of sexual assault who want to reckon with the systems that enabled their assault. To talk about these "non-gospel" things, we are sometimes told, is to distract from the gospel, to create rifts where Christian unity ought to exist. As Christians, we mustn't speak about our differences in heritage or predisposition or experience, and we mustn't

let them show. The gospel is identical for all of us, and therefore we
must be sufficiently identical to receive it.

Amen. Pass the Welch's grape juice and Communion matzo.

But the gospel of uniformity isn't actually good news. Or rather,
it's only good news for the people who already fit the bill, the
people who can be fully honest while also remaining in the majority by every meaningful measure. The rest of us are welcome to
show up at the party too, but only if we wear our name tags selec-
tively. We're asked to hide away the particular bits of ourselves that
look different, sound different, manifest the gospel differently.

The longer you and I hide ourselves away in this belief system,
the harder it becomes to believe that God loves *us* or desires to be
in relationship with *us*. The God we learn to approach is like a
choreographer for the Rockettes, interested in us only to the degree
that we look exactly like the rest of the troupe. Our attempts to
belong within the family of God are constantly thwarted, because
we're trying to belong by impersonating the people we consider
normal enough to be worthy of love.

But God—the real God—has only ever been interested in loving
us, in redeeming *us*, in transforming *us*. He has no interest in an
army of clones, a horde of wax figures and cardboard cutouts sent
to approach him in bold unanimity while his heterogeneous flesh-
and-blood children crouch in the shadows.

Those of us who love Jesus are indeed called to find our para-
mount identity in him. Every other identity is placed in submission
to Christ, upturned and radically reordered by the logic of the
kingdom of God. But our particularities are not erased in the process.
We are not recycled paper, blended into a pulp and recast as a blank
sheet. We are a painted canvas in the hands of a master restorer,
painstakingly cleansed and healed and remade until we finally
become the irreplicable artwork we were always intended to be.

It wasn't until after the fall of humankind that Adam and Eve
learned to play hide and seek, to wear fig leaves like camouflage

and disappear into the landscape. And God in Genesis 3:9 took the role of the seeker, calling out to them as he still calls each of us, no matter how cleverly we try to hide ourselves away: "Where are you?"

The point of the question is not that God needs to know the answer. It is, rather, that Adam and Eve and their descendants need to know the question. God patiently bids us be seen, bids us make ourselves known, even when every bone in our postlapsarian body wishes for anonymity.

○ ○ ○

A handful of friends in college learned the secret of my Indonesian identity (though not my sexual identity) fairly early on. I wasn't sure at first how they would react. Sometimes I worried they might single me out, obsess about my difference, accept me as an object of fascination rather than a friend. Other times, I worried they wouldn't care at all about Indonesia, and I'd feel guilty for bringing it up. In either case, I worried that being known would be an impediment to my belonging.

As it turned out, the opposite was true. The people who knew me best were the ones with whom I belonged most deeply, no matter how different we turned out to be.

Go figure.

A month or two into the fall semester, a few of those friends and I watched the movie *Mean Girls* together. Cady Heron's life wasn't a perfect parallel to mine—she grows up in Africa instead of Indonesia, and returns to the United States for high school instead of college—but the resonances were still impossible to ignore. (We also both thought Aaron Samuels was cute.)

At one point in the movie, Cady meets the airheaded Karen Smith, who asks, "So if you're from Africa, why are you white?" And Karen's friend Gretchen Wieners chides her: "You can't just ask people why they're white."

My delightfully snarky friend Rachael, cozied next to me on the couch, tapped my shoulder. "So if you're from Indonesia," she whispered, giving me a quizzical look, "why are you white?"

"You can't just ask people why they're white," I whispered back.

Still, it was a fair question. Why was I white? What had my whiteness meant for me when I lived in Indonesia, and what did it mean now that I'd entered a nation where my skin color put me in the numeric majority? Were there opportunities or responsibilities that came with being white in this brave new world? Were there corporate sins to repent of, pitfalls to avoid, redemptions to pursue?

Nine years later, I saw delightfully snarky Rachael and her husband Brent at a talk I was giving on faith and sexuality. (Brent had been my roommate during my freshman year of college, so I take at least a modicum of credit for their current marital bliss.) They greeted me with an out-of-context quote from *The Emperor's New Groove*: "Bless you for coming out in public."

It was easy in that moment to wish I'd had the courage to come out to them nine years earlier. Perhaps I could have enjoyed a deeper belonging with them so much sooner than I had. But everything takes time, even when it comes to belonging.

Especially when it comes to belonging.

Back in college, once every six months or so, Rachael would look over at me for no particular reason and furrow her brow. "So," she would say slowly, with a hint of mischief in her voice, "if you're from Indonesia . . . why are you white?"

Gretchen Wieners would have objected, but I was always grateful to be asked.

6

Dengue Days

Notes from an Alien Anthropologist:
Unless the human creatures are forced to confront their own weakness, their self-perception easily becomes distorted. Illness is sometimes a tragedy, but it can also mark a return to sanity.

The uncontrollable shaking began during my orchestration class on Tuesday afternoon. It was bad enough that Dr. Barta, our beloved music theory professor, noticed it from the front of the classroom and interrupted his lecture. "Gregory," he said in his booming *basso profundo* voice, "are you all right?"

"I'm not sure," I answered, my voice trembling every bit as much as the rest of me. "I'll go to the health center after class."

"You'll go to the health center *now*," said Dr. Barta as kindly as possible.

It wasn't until I'd shivered my way into the nurse practitioner's office that I realized the weakness invading my body felt familiar. "You should probably know," I told her at the end of her exam, "I was visiting my family in Indonesia over Christmas break, and I just got back to Rochester four days ago. The last time I remember feeling like this was in eleventh grade, when I got dengue fever in Indonesia."

"I don't know a lot about dengue fever," she said, "and I certainly don't know its incubation period off the top of my head. Let me do some research and get back to you."

Ten minutes later, she called as I was walking to my apartment. "You need to come back in right away. We need to send you to the hospital for some blood tests."

My nurse-in-training friend Kate Wilson—Willie, as I called her—took it upon herself to be my escort to the hospital that evening. I was much weaker than I'd been even a few hours ago, and I leaned on her as we walked. The phlebotomist drew eleven vials of blood from my arm, seeming surprised when I fainted somewhere around the fifth vial. "Stay with me!" she yelled in my ear as my vision turned to static like an old VHS tape. I woke up to the sensation of orange juice being poured into my mouth from a disposable plastic cup.

The next morning, when Willie came to take me for the second round of blood tests, I didn't have the strength to stand upright without help. My temperature had spiked above 103 degrees. "I'm not taking you back to the phlebotomist," she said. "We're going straight to the emergency department."

○ ○ ○

Here were my plans for the spring of 2012: I would finish my senior year of college with a flourish. I would ace all my Greek exams, dazzle my internship supervisor, and manage not to drown in my water polo class. I would lead worship in chapel a few times each month, lead worship for my church's Saturday evening services, and play piano in the Sunday morning services. I would write for the school newspaper, tutor for three different classes, and try to find a literary agent for my first novel.

None of those plans involved spending five days in the hospital and another three weeks on bed rest, missing the first month of the semester. But some things don't need to be planned to become realities.

A team from the Centers for Disease Control and Prevention came to visit me in the emergency department. They scribbled and frowned at their clipboards from inside their face masks, asking questions without appearing to want my answers:

Had I been in any other countries besides Indonesia?

Yes, I stopped off in Qatar during a long layover.

Did I eat any food in Qatar?

Yes, I had some delicious street meat from an open-air market.

What about in Indonesia? Did I eat street food there?

Loads. Obviously.

Did I go into any bodies of water in Indonesia?

Yes, we spent a week at the beach.

What about fresh water?

Yes, I swam along Java's famous Green Canyon.

Had I been near any bats?

Yes, we visited an old World War II–era cave that was full of bats.

The longer I talked, the deeper their frowns grew—even though their mouths were hidden, I could see it in their eyes. Who knew what highly contagious tropical plague I might have smuggled across American borders, a cheap souvenir picked up as I was fraternizing with the bats?

Eventually, to everyone's relief, my doctors decided that dengue fever was a good tentative explanation for my symptoms. The dengue virus is transmitted by mosquito bites, which meant there was no risk of me spreading the disease and starting an epidemic in western New York. Like malaria—dengue's more popular cousin who gets all the attention at parties—dengue can only be spread by certain breeds of mosquito, and those breeds all tend to live in tropical and subtropical parts of the world. Unlike malaria, dengue can't be prevented or treated with medication. (As of 2019, the United States FDA has approved one dengue vaccine, but its use is highly restricted, and it remains only partially effective.)

Dengue is one of those diseases that stays in your blood even after you've recovered. Whereas this lingering effect can give your body immunity in the case of some diseases—think chicken pox,

for example—dengue antibodies have the opposite effect. As soon
as the virus is reintroduced to your body, preexisting antibodies
flare up again in all the wrong ways, meaning that having dengue
a second time is worse than having it once. A third infection, a
fourth infection: with every new roll of the dice, the odds are
weighted toward greater severity and a higher risk of mortality.

I was only on my second infection, which meant the likelihood
of death was still comparatively low. And I certainly wasn't planning
on dying.

But some things don't need to be planned to become realities.

○ ○ ○

I'm one of those people who would like to believe the world relies
on me. If you sat me down next to a hand crank and told me I had
to keep cranking so Planet Earth would keep spinning, I'd take
your word for it. I'd feel secretly pleased, too. I'd sit there self-
importantly, sweating bullets as I cranked, telling anyone who
would listen about how sore my shoulders were getting. But when
they offered to take over and give me a break, I'd refuse. "The pain
is worth it," I would tell them heroically, slapping Band-Aids over
my blisters. "The planet needs me."

For a person like me, there's nothing more humbling than having
the crank taken away and realizing the world still spins just fine in
my absence.

Dengue fever left my brain relatively intact while rendering my
body too weak to act on my brain's ideas. I could make conversation,
but only slowly and softly, fighting for every syllable. Reading took
too much energy, and besides, looking at small print made me
woozy and increased the risk I would vomit again. Recorded music
felt piercing and painful; televisions and computers were out of
the question.

So I did nothing, most of the time. I reclined against my hospital bed, trying to think of anything other than the perpetual pain

gnawing at my bones, feeling cold saline trickle into my arm through an IV needle. I prayed at the same trickling pace as my IV fluid, an unending silent conversation with God, making up in persistence what I lacked in eloquence. I relieved myself in a plastic urinal every few hours, too tired to care when a nurse walked in on me, waving away her apologies with a wry smile. "At the moment," I reassured her, "privacy is low on my priority list."

The lack of privacy cut both ways. Whenever commotion erupted around me, I eavesdropped shamelessly. The middle-schooler with sickle cell anemia, begging for stronger pain medicine. The impatient father asking anyone within earshot what was taking so long. The nurses calling a Code Blue when an overdosed drug addict went into cardiac arrest. The shrieks of the addict's mother reverberating down the hall: "My baby! Jesus, my baby! Oh sweet Jesus, not my baby!" The rattle of the crash cart, the tense murmuring. The mother's wails turning into something like laughter when her son was resuscitated.

Pain. Death. Revival. I bore witness to it all, with no power to do anything more than exist alongside it. The world spun without me.

Two of my supervisors came to visit me in the hospital. Dr. Caton, both a history professor and a Catholic priest, wore his clerical collar so he could ignore normal visitation hours. "I miss my teaching assistant," he said. Tim, my church's worship pastor, caught me up on the latest activities at church. "We miss our piano player," he said.

College friends came to visit, too. They brought pale pink guava juice, which my parents had recommended to them as a popular Indonesian dengue treatment. They brought my Greek textbook, so I could begin studying the moment my pain and nausea subsided. And they brought stories from campus, reports of Twister games and boxed macaroni and cheese eaten late at night. "We miss you," they said.

But life was moving on while I stayed behind. Dr. Caton was inventing ways not to need me for the time being. Tim was finding other pianists, other worship leaders, to fill the musical gap I had left. My friends were carrying on in my absence, living without me in the same fashion we had all grown accustomed to living together.

Some selfish part of me wanted them to do more than miss me. I wanted them to need me. I wanted them to fall apart without me. Fortunately for all of us, they didn't.

○ ○ ○

Rochester, New York, is not known for its high incidence of dengue fever. I was highly favored among the medical students and residents, who crowded into my room to hear reports on my progress, salivating over me like I was rare exotic cuisine.

"Do you mind some extra company?" one of my doctors politely asked before the first flock of med students arrived. "If you'd prefer more privacy, I completely understand. But you'd be a great teaching opportunity."

"I might as well contribute to society while I'm sitting here like a lump," I said. "Bring on the party."

A med student named Vince, in the final year of his MD/PhD program, became my steady conversation partner, getting updates on my progress a few times every day. I told him about Indonesia, about my pain level, about the conjugation of Greek verbs, about my bowel movements or lack thereof. When I pooped for the first time in over a week, Vince proudly reported this news to a roomful of attentive doctors and med students, who gave me an ovation. (I haven't once been applauded for pooping since. So much achievement left unsung.)

Once my skin had regained its usual color and I no longer seemed at risk of dying, they transferred me to an inpatient wing. "Welcome to the fourth floor," said the nurse who greeted me. "We have a lot of fun up here. We also have earplugs."

A thin curtain separated me from my new roommate, Manny. He had been admitted for alcohol poisoning, and a patient-care tech stayed with him around the clock. Sometimes Manny would pontificate about the nature of the afterlife or the reasons his wife left him. Sometimes he would yell to be released, tugging at the restraints that held him against his bed. "Sir," the patient care tech would say wearily, "please don't pull on your Foley catheter. Sir, if you pull out your Foley, you'll tear your urethra, and then you'll have much bigger problems."

I wore the earplugs.

○ ○ ○

No one had told me that the Christmas of my senior year of college would be my last visit to Indonesia. But in the three weeks I was there, I couldn't shake the nagging feeling that I was saying goodbye. Call it a premonition, if you will, or God's gracious revelation, or just an (un)lucky guess. Whatever it was, the feeling clung to me, like I was making a final hospital visit to a dying friend.

Everything I saw in those three weeks, I saw with the awareness that I might never see it again on this side of heaven. I walked my favorite neighborhood trails, drank young coconut milk from a plastic bag, ate greasy pan-fried *martabak* filled with chocolate and peanuts. I spent time in the kitchen with Ibu Herni, the Indonesian woman who had been my longest-standing cooking companion. When I hugged her goodbye, my six-foot-three-inch body folded over her short frame as she squeezed me at the waist. Both of us pretended we weren't crying. "*Sampai nanti*," she said, clasping my hands between hers, and I returned the words: "Until later."

I put the pieces together in the emergency room. A few days later, other people started speaking them out loud. "We recommend that you avoid going back to parts of the world where dengue is endemic," said my doctors. "A third infection might not have the same happy ending this one did."

"Why risk it?" said my professors. "You can do plenty of good here in the global north."

"Don't worry about visiting us anymore," said my parents. "We'll visit you."

The realization didn't come as a shock. It felt less like a punch to the gut and more like the appearance of a bruise, a slow-acting pain that I'd been anticipating. I *could* still go back to Indonesia, of course—I had no objection to risking my life if the Lord called in that direction—but barring a clear sense of calling, it seemed foolhardy to play the odds. There would be no more nostalgia-motivated visits home.

"What an awful thing to happen," people sometimes tell me when they hear the story. "What a tragedy."

But when I remember back to the dengue days, despite their inescapable ongoing sorrow, I can't help thinking of them with fondness.

I think of how each of my professors worked with me to ensure that I graduated on time, even after I had missed four weeks of class. I think of the kindness of strangers like Vince the med student, like the woman in the emergency department waiting area who asked Willie what was wrong with me and then began blessing me with a loud charismatic prayer: "Calm his system, Jesus! Calm his system!"

I think of the friends who came to visit me in the hospital, of how my brother John and sister-in-law Heather drove two-and-a-half hours just to play cards and watch me eat packages of graham crackers in my light blue hospital-chic pajamas. I think of Willie and other volunteer caregivers taking my temperature, tracking my ibuprofen consumption, forcing water down my throat. I think of phone calls to my roommates in the middle of the night when I was too weak to walk, waking them up to enlist their help as I hobbled to the bathroom.

I think of how no one is deserted when community functions as it was designed to function.

The helplessness of dengue fever is the closest I've come in adulthood (so far) to the helplessness of the womb. There was nothing I could try harder at, nothing I could earn. And yet, somehow, my worth remained undiminished. The God at the other end of my trickling prayers caught every last droplet, answering them with a thundering peace that saturated me like a rainstorm. I was loved. At the height of neediness, of uselessness, I was loved. Even if I never sang or wrote or spoke or earned taxable income again, I would still be loved.

When I finally made it out of the hospital, off bed rest, back to normal life, I almost missed being sick. I missed the vivid clarity, the obviousness of my absolute dependence on God and others. I had come to recognize the beauty of life with dengue, of belonging without earning, of letting the world spin without claiming responsibility for it. In a strange way, I had grown to love my dengue days.

Still, I wasn't meant to stay in the hospital forever. My post-dengue life was full of new beauty. The beauty of eating food, of walking to the bathroom by my own strength, of not being in constant pain. The beauty of returning to piano keys and computer keys, setting words and melodies to the affection pooling in my heart. The beauty of giving myself away, of serving others instead of just being served by them.

My dengue days were only a temporary gift, a season meant to prepare the way for the seasons that followed. And sure enough, I lived differently in the days and months and years after my hospitalization. I prayed differently, hoped differently, believed differently.

Would it be so unfair if my fifteen years in Indonesia had been the same? A temporary gift, a home with an expiration date, a season meant to prepare the way for the seasons that followed?

Beauty, we are told in Ecclesiastes 3, is a seasonal matter, one beauty passing away to plant the seeds for another. Everything has been made beautiful in its time—not a moment longer, not a moment less. Including the seasons we wish had never begun. Including the seasons we wish could last forever.

Beauty accomplishes its mission even in the moment it departs. Even when it clasps our hands in its own and says, "*Sampai nanti. Until later.*"

How to Deal Drugs

Notes from an Alien Anthropologist:
The greater the promised reward, the more a human creature will risk to bring it about. To change humans' attitudes toward the present, simply change their attitudes toward the future.

I clutched the wad of cash in my hand tightly. It was thirty bills deep, all Andrew Jacksons. A cool $600 in paper.

No one on the busy downtown sidewalk was paying much attention to me, but I felt exposed all the same. I hurried back to my car, parallel-parked beside a meter blinking the word *expired*. The moment I'd gotten inside and closed the door behind me, I pushed a black button on my keys, breathing a sigh of relief as four locks snapped loudly into place.

I counted the money again, slippery against my sweaty fingers. Still $600. The wallet in the back pocket of my jeans had another two twenties, a five, and two ones. I took out the twenties and added them to my stack. $640. It was barely enough.

I had the money.

It was time for my first drug deal.

○ ○ ○

As a kid, whenever I was left alone with a new closet or wardrobe, I would reach in to feel its back wall, hoping I might get sucked into another world the way Lucy Pevensie had stumbled into

Narnia in C. S. Lewis's classic chronicles. Alas, my hand met solid
plywood (or perhaps flimsy, badly nailed cardboard) every time.
But I never stopped looking for centaurs and satyrs and umbrella-
carrying fauns greeting me in a snowy forest. I never stopped believing there was magic waiting for me somewhere, just out of reach.

I've talked with so many others who share this sentiment, this
sense of otherworldly longing. It might not be Narnia they think
of first, but their feet are itching for a place they've never been before.

Sometimes they're waiting for their Hogwarts letter to arrive.

Sometimes they're filing visa applications to Wakanda or
hoping a radioactive spider bite will transform them into Marvel's
next Avenger.

Sometimes they're dreaming of a Twilight romance with a scintillating vampire or a werewolf beefcake.

Sometimes they're hunting for a black-cloaked Morpheus to
offer them the red pill, rescue them from the matrix, and show
them the universe as it really is.

You could call us all "escapist," I suppose, for our eagerness to
discover a new reality intersecting our current one. But I'm not sure
it's escape, per se, that we're longing for. Instead of fleeing *from*
something, I think we're searching *for* something, pining after an
impossibly better world. Homesick for a home that was lost before
we were born.

I think we're homesick for the Garden of Eden.

Adam and Eve no doubt felt this homesickness most acutely.
They could still remember with visceral immediacy what perfection
felt like, what it looked like, what it sounded and smelled and
tasted like. Imagine the stories they must have told their children
about their first homeland: the fantastical world where work was
joy, where pain hadn't been invented, where the air always smelled
like baking bread and old library books and freshly mown grass.
Imagine how they must have longed for the country they were born
into. Imagine their wistful memories of the Edenic property rights

and citizenship they had exchanged for a few enticing bites of mango. (John Milton says in *Paradise Lost* that the forbidden fruit, the price of Eden, was an apple. But who in their right mind would get so excited about an apple? A perfectly ripe mango may still be a bad trade for the eternal happiness of the human race, but it's at least marginally more believable.)

You and I may not have Adam and Eve's firsthand memories of Eden. But just because we never lived there doesn't mean we can't be homesick too. We were designed for that perfect Garden, our hearts and minds and bodies programmed to belong there. Outside of Eden, it's only logical that every other terrain would feel strange beneath our feet, that every other nation's anthem would feel strange on our lips. Perhaps our wishes for another world are just wistful memories inherited from our ancestors.

Why shouldn't our souls—and soles—be anxious to return to the beckoning dirt of the Garden we were made for?

○ ○ ○

Everything had begun innocently enough. I was in town to visit my future graduate program, Penn State's MA/PhD in English. As long as I was in Pennsylvania, I figured I ought to do some apartment hunting, so I set up appointments with three different rental offices in the State College area.

The first apartment complex I visited, which also boasted the cheapest rental rates of the three, showed me an apartment I loved. It was a studio/efficiency setup, everything cozied into one room, with the kitchen in a nook at one corner and the bed beside the window at the opposite corner. The room was half underground, its chest-high window looking out on my neighbors' feet passing in the grass. (In the first few days after I moved into that apartment, I would forget how easily passersby could see into my room. I made the mistake of changing clothes in view of the open window, exposing myself to an unsuspecting neighbor. We both froze for a shocked half-second, after which I bolted into the bathroom. That neighbor and I never became close personal friends.)

"I like it," I told the rental office. "I want to live here."

"Great," they said. "This is the only efficiency we have left, and we're scheduled to show it to another prospective renter in an hour. Do you want to put down a security deposit to claim it before then?"

"Definitely," I said, offering them my credit card.

"Cash or check," they said apologetically.

"Of course," I said. "Let me just get my checkbook—"

At that moment, I realized I knew the exact location of my checkbook. It was safely stowed in my room, a modest six-and-a-half-hour drive north.

Crap.

I went out to my car, where I called my brother John and explained the situation. "How do I write a check for $635 when I don't have a checkbook?" I said.

"Why not pay in cash?" he said.

"There's no way I have $635 in my wallet," I said. "Who carries that much cash?"

"An ATM," said John, without missing a beat.

That thought hadn't occurred to me. I mulled it over for a moment before answering. "Am I allowed to withdraw that much from an ATM all at once?"

"It sounds like you're about to find out," he said.

I followed my phone's navigation system to the nearest ATM, on a downtown street two miles away. When I punched $635 into the machine, it beeped back an error message: "Your daily withdrawal limit is $600."

I rechecked the money in my wallet. It would be enough.

Barely.

"Is this crazy?" I had asked John on the phone just before we hung up. "What if I end up maxing out my debit card and emptying my wallet? Twenty minutes ago I didn't even know this apartment existed, and now I might be expending all the resources I have for it."

"As long as you get the apartment," said John in his older-brotherly wisdom, "it's not crazy at all."

With seven dollars left in my wallet and no way of replenishing the supply, I drove back to the rental office. I slunk inside, carrying the largest stack of money I had ever held. "I realize this looks like a drug deal," I told the bemused staff. "But I promise you it's not."

o o o

In Matthew 13:44, Jesus tells a parable of a man discovering hidden treasure in a field. The man sells everything he owns to buy the field. He empties his wallet and his bank account, hawks his most prized possessions on eBay, and then spends the whole wad of cash on a patch of dirt. He becomes a momentary pauper.

If there's no treasure in the field, he's crazy. Foolhardy. Irresponsible. Pitiable.

But if there is treasure, he's not crazy at all.

Seven chapters earlier, in the Sermon on the Mount, Jesus had already counseled his followers on how to think about their treasure: "Do not store up for yourselves treasures on earth, where moths and vermin destroy, and where thieves break in and steal. But store up for yourselves treasures in heaven, where moths and vermin do not destroy, and where thieves do not break in and steal. For where your treasure is, there your heart will be also" (Matthew 6:19-21).

In both passages, Jesus' point has to do with thinking ahead, playing the long game. If we're only paying attention to our earthly existence—ordering our lives and expending our resources to maximize our well-being in this lifetime—we'll never invest ourselves fully in the kingdom of heaven.

Notice that, by emphasizing heaven, Jesus isn't trying to make people pay *less* attention to the way they live on earth. He's not asking his followers to become, as the saying goes, "so heavenly minded that they are no earthly good." Jesus is declaring that people can only live truly selfless, self-giving lives on earth once they come to believe that their own earthly wealth and happiness are not the point of the story. The radical generosity to which Jesus calls his followers—giving to the poor and needy, loving our enemies, valuing other people's needs and interests above our own—will only make sense to us if our eyes are set on a greater treasure.

Laying up our treasures in heaven means that we can afford to give them away for now. Instead of making us worse inhabitants of earth, the thought of heaven ought to make us the most generous, most selfless people on the planet.

On the other hand, if we can't see far enough into the future to gamble everything on that coming treasure, we'll waste our resources and energies trying to take care of ourselves, trying to bring about our own happy endings. We'll spend our time and money and passions on fleeting earthly things, acting like citizens of the planet instead of like Jesus-obsessed aliens.

The way we live in the present moment depends on the things we believe about the future. And those who belong to Jesus' kingdom live with an otherworldly future in mind. They deposit their treasure into heavenly bank accounts, knowing their feet will never reach home until they return to Eden's soil. They live like people who might stumble into Narnia at any moment.

○ ○ ○

A. J. Swoboda, in his exquisite book *A Glorious Dark*, describes the awkward, uncertain waiting that comes between Jesus' death and his resurrection. The bitter dashed hopes of the disciples. The weight of Jesus' body as Joseph of Arimathea carries it to the tomb. The storm clouds and tears. The darkness inside the tomb, where the stench of death feels so much more certain than the promise of life. The haunting, unbroken silence.

The temptation for so many of us, as Swoboda rightly diagnoses, is to bypass the waiting, to skip over Holy Saturday altogether and jump straight to the story's happy ending. We don't like waiting. We don't like the heavy, holy darkness. Everyone wants to be carried by Jesus, but no one wants to sign up with Joseph of Arimathea to carry him.

Yet so much of our life of faith exists in the middle space, in the season when glory feels impossibly heavy, in the waiting between the promise and its fulfillment. The road to eternity inevitably passes through the valley of the shadow of death. If our treasure is stowed away in New Narnian coffers, we might look like paupers for a little while on earth. And that's okay.

Paupers aren't really paupers when they're just waiting to inherit a fortune. They may have empty wallets and maxed-out debit cards for a day. But as long as they get the apartment, it's not crazy at all.

There's a kind of homelessness in the waiting between the first Eden and the second Eden. But it's not so impossible to belong like an alien in the meantime, once you know what you're waiting for.

"In the tomb," Swoboda writes, "the darkness is thick. But that's where God is."

A Glorious Dark

(with a hat tip to A. J. Swoboda)

Calloused and dusty feet
Wandering foreign earth
Searching for Eden's garden soil
Stolen before your birth
Every desire you chase
Pales against Eden's own
Beauty gone wrong cannot belong
Till you are finally home

Hands that have borne our Hope
Laying him in the grave
Grasping at Eden's fallen leaves
As they are blown away
Glory must have its weight
Hidden by tomb and stone
Three midnights mark a glorious dark
Till you are finally home

Bleeding and broken heart
Be not afraid to beat
Hear how the resurrection drum
Rises from love's defeat
Sorrow will yield to sky
Grave will give way to throne
Each tear it cries, love satisfies
Till you are finally home

PART TWO

Belonging With

Yet everything that touches us, me and you,
takes us together like a violin's bow,
which draws one voice out of two separate strings.
Upon what instrument are we two spanned?
And what musician holds us in his hand?

Rainer Maria Rilke

8

A Jedi's Training

Notes from an Alien Anthropologist:
The human creatures are always trying to change the rate at which time passes. But Planet Earth spins at a consistent rate, regardless of their preferences, and this movement keeps them alive.

In my earliest memories of Zack Filbert, we are already best friends. As far as Young Greg was concerned, nothing had existed prior to our friendship. We had never been strangers. There was no getting-to-know-you phase. Zack was intrinsic: as familiar as a native language, as much a part of me as a last name. "Zack-and-Greg," people called us, a single public entity bonded by hyphens.

According to most personality tests, we were practically interchangeable: two amiable, conflict-avoidant, introverted little brothers with an incorrigible creative streak. We invented a secret alphabet and wrote each other coded letters on printer paper dyed with tea to look "historical." We crafted board games out of cereal boxes, Zack taking charge of visual design while I handled the words. We play-acted make-believe scenarios, sometimes enlisting Zack's little sister Krissy as our third character, once devising a detective story so realistic (to us) that we spooked ourselves and had to quit playing.

Yards were a precious commodity in Indonesia, and Zack had two of them. (My own house, by comparison, had no yard to speak of. There was a rectangle of dirt in the front of the house, about fifteen square feet, just large enough for a pine tree and a pomegranate tree and some scraggly bushes. Where the back yard should have been, we had a graveyard instead, rows of ceramic tiled graves with holes in the middle that our neighbors believed would let the spirits of the dead escape after burial.)

In Zack's front yard we played tag and British Bulldog with Krissy and our older brothers John and Nate. When the cloves on the clove tree ripened, we picked them into plastic grocery bags, dried them in the sun, and sold them to our parents' coworkers. The back yard was enclosed by a high concrete wall with a tree fort built up against one corner. John and Nate declared themselves the leaders of an exclusive club that met in the tree fort. To join the club, Zack and I were required to drink a special beverage devised by Nate, a concoction of grape juice and pancake batter and pepper. Like dutiful younger brothers, we drank it.

Anything to belong.

o o o

Zack and I were in eighth grade when his family moved to the United States. I mourned the loss like a funeral. North America, as far as I was concerned, was roughly equivalent to the "Big Farm Up North" where sick pets go to live after their final veterinary appointment. It was a dream world, a place human beings could visit on occasion but were not meant to permanently inhabit.

The move to the United States spelled the end of the Zack-and-Greg era. Never had I been so brokenhearted over the loss of a few hyphens. I cried almost every time I thought about it, which turned out to be a dehydrating habit.

It was even worse for Zack, of course. This was how I chided myself, fiercely, between my tears: "He's the one who has to live in America." (The horror!) "He's the one saying goodbye to *all* his friends. I'm only saying goodbye to one person."

The departure was announced in seventh grade, which left us a whole year of goodbyes before Zack disappeared. A whole year of doing meaningless things together one last time and imbuing them with immeasurable meaning.

We wandered the same narrow neighborhood alleys we had wandered countless times before, giving names to all the landmarks so we could remember them together. One open sewer outlet that always gushed brown water became known as "Chocolate Falls." We named an especially narrow squeeze between buildings "Fat Man's Misery," and an alley covered by a long low-hanging roof became "Tall Man's Agony." The landmark names were typed into a word processing document decorated with garish clip art. Something we could push "save" on and preserve forever.

In our quest for permanence, we resolved to make a movie together. Movies, after all, are things that happen once and then remain fixed into perpetuity. The people in movies aren't subject to the vicissitudes of time. We brainstormed a quick script, enlisted Nate as our cameraman and Krissy as our multipurpose extra, and set about making ourselves immortal.

Our Star Wars fan fiction movie (running time: twenty-seven minutes) was titled *A Jedi's Training*. A Jedi Master (played by Zack) was educating a young Padawan (yours truly) in the mystical ways of the Force. In each scene, the Jedi Master would train the Padawan in a new technique of the Force, and the Padawan would accidentally injure the Master using that same technique: making objects fly through the air and hit the Master, crushing the Master in a sliding doorway, choking the Master instead of the practice dummy, electrocuting the Master instead of the practice dummy. (The dummy was played by Krissy, who held a smiley face beach ball in front of her head. Even with her face hidden, she stole the show.)

Our plot was highly repetitious, but that didn't trouble me much as a young screenwriter. If anything, repetition was a bonus.

I *wanted* a story that would go nowhere and do nothing, only repeat itself day after day, year after year. I wanted a life full of characters who never changed or matured or left the screen. If I could have, I would have poured water over Zack and myself, over the trampoline in the front yard and the rabbit hutch in the backyard, and frozen us solid forever.

Of course, in tropical countries like Indonesia, it's impossible to keep ice from melting.

I savored the final weeks with Zack like a rich dessert, each bite held in the mouth until it disintegrated, knowing I'd be down to the crumbs before long. All too soon, the plate was empty.

o o o

Eleven-and-a-half years later, everything and nothing had changed.

The Filberts survived the move to the United States—and four years down the line, so did I. Nate started going by Nathanael. Krissy metamorphosed from an adorable tiny child into a still-adorable and still-tiny adult. Zack and I grew taller by eight or ten inches apiece: I became skinny for the first time, and Zack advanced from already skinny to invisible-when-turned-sideways.

We grew up in other ways too. Zack's design skills got more sophisticated, and I learned how to write plots that didn't recycle the same gimmick fifteen times. Both of us went to college, spent a year in the work force, started and finished master's degrees. We both gained some confidence. We both dated (he more successfully than I). We both dreamed of a hundred different possible futures.

And through it all, we were friends. Best friends, even.

Much to our young adult chagrin, *A Jedi's Training* kept our youth forever contemporary. Our siblings and friends would threaten to watch it every time we got together. Whenever they made good on their threats, Zack and I would laugh and groan through the viewing party. "Look at us!" we would say. "Listen to my voice! Who wrote this script? Why did we think this was a good idea?"

Eleven-and-a-half years later, you couldn't have paid me enough to return to my thirteen-year-old self and live in eternal puberty. I had no desire to trade in my present-day friendship with Zack for my former friendship with Zack. We were deeper friends as the years went on, because there were more years and more memories binding us together. My old fantasy of freezing the world in place seemed foolish and juvenile.

Then Zack got married.

I met Anna, his future wife, during a weekend trip to a lake house along Lake Erie. It didn't even take the whole weekend to make me a believer. They were wonderful together, quirky in complementary ways. Zack had a new vitality when he was with Anna, something fresh and different and yet still thoroughly himself. I wanted to be friends with her, and I wanted him to get married, and I wanted him to marry her. All boxes ticked. Put a ring on it and call it a day.

He put a ring on it. I was pleased.

And yet.

I cried at Zack and Anna's wedding like I've never cried at a wedding before or since. There I was in the groomsmen's lineup, hands dutifully clasped left over right, every muscle in my face tensed to keep my tear ducts at least marginally obedient.

"You looked so serious," my brother John told me after the ceremony. "I've never seen you look so serious."

"Marriage is a big deal," I said, both accurately and evasively.

My raw emotions had something to do, I'm sure, with the fact that I had come out as gay two days ago, quite by accident, to Zack and Nathanael during Zack's bachelor party. We had talked about how I expected to probably stay celibate for life. And so, on Zack's wedding day, Zack and Nathanael and I all knew as we stood side by side what only one of us had known a week prior: That every promise Zack made to Anna at the altar was a promise I might never make to anyone. That I couldn't just follow Zack into married life as readily as I'd followed him to the United States. That for the second time in our lives, Zack was embarking on a new adventure and leaving me behind.

People are supposed to cry at weddings because of sheer happiness. And we do, of course. I certainly did. I cried because I was happy for Zack, because I wanted him and Anna to be together, because I reckoned myself a part of their adventure in some vicarious, best friend sort of way. I cried because sometimes spectacular things are worthy of our tears of delight.

But I think some of us also cry at weddings for the loss of the world as we know it right now. Marriage, however great it may be, makes things different. It makes people different. And though we hope and pray that people's marital selves will be an improvement on their premarital selves, we already love the people we love exactly as they are.

We cry, even if it's selfish, because we're saying goodbye to the here-and-now we adore so much. We cry because some small part of us still wants to douse the world in water and freeze it in place forever. Forget growth; forget expiration dates; forget freezer burn. If I belong with you, then I want you to keep being what you've always been to me, so that I can keep belonging with you like I always have.

Just stay. Hold still.

o o o

Maybe this is one reason love sometimes smothers, one reason people sometimes sabotage the friendships they value most. Maybe we keep buying into the fantasy that our dearest relationships can thrive in immobility. We wrap our fingers around the present and hold too tightly, choking it even as it swells and blossoms into the future.

o o o

The year after Zack and Anna's wedding, I spent Thanksgiving with them in their cozy Chicago apartment. (By "cozy," I mean that we got our privacy mostly during bathroom visits.) None of us had ever been in charge of a Thanksgiving feast before, so we took on the responsibility collaboratively, googling our way through the turkey roasting, calling mothers and emailing grandmothers for side dish recipes and tips.

Nathanael came over after the feasting to partake in a time-honored Filbert brothers' Thanksgiving tradition: watching all three of the Lord of the Rings films. The extended editions. "Over eleven hours of cinematic genius," as Nathanael said.

I don't dislike the Lord of the Rings films. Neither does Anna. But both of us, by virtue of our proximity to the Filbert family, had already seen the whole trilogy on multiple occasions. The extended editions. Over eleven hours of cinematic genius.

We made it through the first two films without incident, one on Thanksgiving night, one the next morning. But when the time came for *The Return of the King*, Anna looked at me with desperate eyes.

"I don't think I'm going to make it," she said.

I felt similarly. But we couldn't just hide in the bathroom for the next four hours. I proposed a game of bingo.

"Bingo?" Anna looked at me incredulously.

"Bingo," I said.

As the movie began, we divided two sheets of paper into bingo grids and made a list of twenty-five events that might happen during the film. Some of our entries were cinemato-graphic: "Elf speaks in whispery tone." "Dwarf provides comic relief." "Minor character dies by decapitation." Others had to do with the behaviors of our viewing companions: "Nathanael sings along with the soundtrack." "Zack quotes a line right before the movie character says it."

We kept our bingo board entries secret from the rest of the room, whispering to each other conspiratorially on the couch. Barely

more than twenty minutes into the movie, a tender scene made
Nathanael cozy up against his girlfriend, Sam, who had joined us
for the evening. Anna and I burst out gleefully as we marked our
bingo boards: "Movie moment inspires physical affection between
Nathanael and Sam."

"Wait," said everyone else, "what are you guys doing?"

And on it went. We spent a hefty chunk of the battle scenes
deliberating over what counted as "impalement." Technically, I got
bingo at around the two-hour mark, but we kept playing anyway,
whispering conspiratorially for the sheer pleasure of the conspiratorial bond. By the end of the film, we had only one bingo square
left unmarked: Zack had never gotten up and started dancing to
the music (though we became increasingly brazen in our attempts
to egg him on).

When the closing credits ran, Anna turned to me in the glowing
half-dark. "I've never enjoyed the Lord of the Rings so much."

I nodded. "I don't think I can watch them any other way."

During my drive home from Chicago, I thought of all the times
I had watched the Lord of the Rings with Nathanael and Zack in
the years before Anna. I thought of old Thanksgivings spent with
the Filberts, of how easily I had always felt at home with them. I
thought of the married man I called my best friend, back when he
was still a boy, back when we were just two aspiring Jedi with a
video camera.

I thought of all the times I had longed to freeze the world in
place. Of all the times I had said, *Hold still, so I can belong with
you forever.*

Then I thought of Anna. The cozy apartment. The collaborative
turkey. The conspiratorial whispering. The best bingo game of my life.

Speeding along a frigid Indiana highway, I offered up a prayer
of thanks for a world that keeps melting through my fingers.

9

Santai Sundays

Notes from an Alien Anthropologist:
Some of the human creatures play a quaint game called "Keeping the Friendship Alive," in which they make themselves and each other feel guilty for not spending more time together even when they have no time to spend.

The feeling of being a TCK is the feeling of always missing someone," my friend Carrie tells me as we sit at a picnic table outside a Pennsylvania gas station.

By TCK, Carrie means a "third-culture kid": a child born to parents of one culture, raised in a second culture, and thus eking out a hybrid third culture that incorporates but also exceeds the first two. She's talking about kids who can't figure out which continent "home" is supposed to be on. Kids whose closest friends might live hundreds or thousands of miles away in multiple directions. Kids who love so many different people and places that they can't possibly hope to see them all again on this side of heaven.

In other words, she's talking about the two of us.

Carrie and her younger brother, Evan, grew up with me in Indonesia. For most of our childhoods, they lived three hours away from my family, in the same town as our mutual friends Sarah and Hannah. But at least once or twice a year, all our parents would get together for work meetings at a hotel somewhere, and the kids would spend hours swimming, followed by additional hours playing card games while sitting cross-legged atop hotel mattresses. In between parental meetings, we planned visits to see each other whenever we could—cajoling our parents into driving us between cities, or taking the train when no parents could be cajoled.

Because our extended families all lived in the United States, none of us saw our blood relatives regularly. But we called each other's parents "aunt" and "uncle," and we became close the way cousins become close in some families. We weren't like regular friends, the kind who live close by and see each other often and share life's ongoing minutiae. We sometimes went without contact for months or even years at a time. But whenever we had the good fortune to be together again, we always picked up right where we left off. No matter how much time passed between our hangouts, our friendships never seemed to dissolve.

No one ever stops being cousins.

It was because of me, at least partially, that Carrie and Evan moved to central Pennsylvania. After spending three post-college years working on the Indonesian island of Batam, Carrie decided to come back to the United States and apply to graduate programs in counseling. She could have lived anywhere that first year, while she was in the throes of grad school applications. But I used my impressive rhetorical skill (or so I'd like to believe) to persuade her that she might as well move to State College and apply to the counseling program at Penn State.

"If you get accepted and decide to go to Penn State," I told her, "you won't need to move again next year. Besides, you could live in the same town as me."

"*Abang*," said Carrie, calling me the Indonesian name for an older brother, "that would be fabulous."

Not long afterward, Carrie was on the phone with Evan, who explained to her that he was wishing for a new job and a fresh start in life. Carrie persuaded him with the same brilliant argument that had persuaded her: "You should just move to State College with me. We could live in the same town as *Abang* Greg."

And so, mere months later, Carrie and Evan moved into an apartment on the same street as me. Before the move, I hadn't seen either of them in over a year. We'd spent most of our lives in different Indonesian provinces, different American states, or different countries altogether. Suddenly, we were only a six-minute walk apart.

It takes some adjustment, we quickly learned, living close to someone you've mostly seen on vacations and at special events. Under other circumstances, we would have been inseparable, trying to squeeze every last drop out of our time together before parting ways for another season of relational drought. But none of us had the time—or the emotional stamina—to be together nonstop in State College. I was in my fifth year of grad school, writing a dissertation and promoting a recently published book in my "spare" time. Carrie was nannying for three different families, picking up shifts at Target, and writing endless admissions essays. Evan was recovering from ACL surgery and polishing his résumé as he crutched his way from temp job to temp job.

"It's ridiculous, *Abang*," Carrie told me one Sunday after church. "We live so close, but we never see each other."

"I know," I said. "There's so much work to do. And when we're not working, it's hard to have energy left for anything else."

"You could come over this afternoon," said Carrie. "We don't have to do anything that takes energy. We can just *santai-santai*."

Santai means "relaxed" in Indonesian, and the phrase *santai-santai* translates roughly to "chill out." *Santai* is also pronounced quite a bit like the English word *Sunday*.

"*Santai* Sunday?" I said with a smirk.

Carrie fixed me with a disapproving stare. "No, *Abang*. Not *Santai* Sunday. *Santai-santai*."

But my tongue-in-cheek name stuck. In the following weeks and months, *Santai* Sundays became part of the regular rhythm of our lives, as long as I was in town that weekend and no one had other compelling obligations.

On *Santai* Sundays, there were no fixed rules. Some weeks we invited other friends over to join us, coaxing them to sample our favorite Indonesian drinks and candies, with Evan translating for our guests whenever Carrie and I started speaking to each other in Indonesian. Other weeks it was just me and Carrie and Evan, reading books or napping on the couch or tapping away at our computers or playing the same card games we'd played when we were kids. Some weeks we made complex dinners together, grinding cloves of garlic and bright purple shallots with a mortar and pestle, thinly slicing still more shallots and deep frying them into a crispy topping for *nasi goreng*, Indonesian-style fried rice. Other weeks we kept it simple, buttering slices of whole wheat toast and eating omelets dappled with frozen vegetables.

Guests or no guests, we always changed out of our church clothes and into comfy clothes, the kind with stains and holes in them. If my voice was especially tired from leading worship that morning, I would drink licorice root tea and talk sparingly. None of us was trying to impress anyone else with our fashion choices or party planning skills or vibrant personalities. None of us was *trying* at all. We were simply existing. We were *santai-santai* together, our public faces laid to rest, chilling out in each other's company. We were the kind of friends who didn't need to be impressed by each other.

No one ever stops being cousins.

○ ○ ○

The feeling of being a TCK is the feeling of always missing someone. The longer I live, the worse the problem becomes. It was bad enough in childhood, when I had one scatterplot of friends on multiple Indonesian islands and another scatterplot in multiple American states. Then my childhood friends dispersed around the globe, and I moved to Rochester, where I made still more friends in college. Then *those* friends dispersed, and I moved to Potsdam, and . . . well, you get the idea. I love an inconvenient number of people.

"They can't *really* all still be your friends," a pessimistic friend told me recently. "Facebook friends, maybe, or acquaintances you enjoy. But friends have to spend regular time together. Friendship takes work. You've got to have bimonthly phone calls and send birthday cards and know when they remodel their kitchen."

In my experience, my pessimistic friend is at least partially correct, in the following two ways: First, human beings absolutely need the kinds of friends with whom we spend regular time, the people who share our lives' quotidian moments. We need people who come alongside us, and people whom we come alongside, in the regular day-to-day, witnessing our joys and sorrows and successes and failures. Otherwise, we're set up for unhealthy isolation. Solomon makes the point well in Ecclesiastes 4: "Two are better than one, because they have a good return for their labor: If either of them falls down, one can help the other up. But pity anyone who falls and has no one to help them up." (This passage often gets read aloud at weddings, to illustrate how splendid marriage is. Far be it from me to deprive the romantics of their fun, but it seems worth noting that Solomon's prelude to this sentiment reads, "There was a man all alone; he had neither son nor brother." Marriage may not be entirely excluded from view here as a form of companionship, but it's certainly not the only—or even the primary—form of companionship in Solomon's mind.)

So yes, we need friends whose lives are naturally tangled up in our own. But I would contend that not all of our friends need to play that role, not all the time. Just because *someone* needs to bear witness to our daily realities doesn't mean that *everyone* must.

Second, some friendships do indeed rely on regular time together in order to keep existing. These friendships, in my observation, are the ones that focus mostly or exclusively on everyday things. They're about having fun and staying connected—both of which are good aspirations—but there's little sense of shared passion or greater common purpose to make them resilient. Because the relationship is only skin deep, all it takes is one good exfoliation before it disappears. Someone gets busy, or someone leaves town without maintaining a robust correspondence, and suddenly the friendship has evaporated.

I've chosen to live by the rude and unpopular policy that it's okay to let skin-deep friendships fade away.

To be clear, I don't think there's anything wrong with having these sorts of friendships. Sometimes they do eventually permeate the epidermis and get into the bloodstream. And even if they never get deep, I think it's okay to have shallow friends, friends who are simply fun to be around in the season they are gifted to us.

But if we constantly feel the pressure to keep watering every friendship we've ever had in order to keep them all alive, we'll eventually have to stop making new friends in order to not exhaust our water supply. We'll be stuck in the past, investing so much time keeping up with old friends that we forget to love the people God has put in front of us for the present season.

I have so many friends who feel constantly guilty of being a "bad friend" to others. When I quiz them about their badness, it turns out that they're guilty of not regularly getting together or staying in touch with all the friends they've accrued over the years. "Is it even humanly possible," I asked one such friend as we were washing dishes together, "for you to keep up all the correspondence you feel like you should be keeping up? And if you did, would you still have time to do your own work and hang out with all the people you love in this town? And if you did that, would you still have time to sleep?"

"No," she sighed.

"So what you're saying is that you want to get rid of some friends?" I asked with a smirk. "Eliminate the mediocre ones?"

She threw a well-deserved dish towel at me. "Of course not!"

"Then it sounds like you might need to start trusting that the friends who matter most won't stop being your friends when you're not in contact with each other. And if some of your shallow friendships wither away, you might have to be okay with that too."

Our truest friendships can endure through seasons of silence and absence. They're like camels, storing up enough water to last for long spells in the desert. Camels still need water, of course. But they're not fragile. They don't demand constant attention.

The family status of cousins is never under threat, no matter how far apart the family reunions fall. And if we take Jesus' words about the family of God seriously, then we are amply stocked with cousins. We are united to one another by the immovable reality of our shared relationship to the King of heaven. The bloodlines that hold us together are divine promises far thicker than blood.

Certainly, we shouldn't take advantage of this fact to ignore our dearest friends. Quite the opposite. When we stop feeling obligated to keep our friendships alive, they become more restful, more joyous, more life-giving. Instead of perpetually pouring energy into one another, we become able to be *santai* together. Phone calls and visits, when they happen, feel like lavish gifts instead of strict obligations. We invest in and strengthen our friendships, not out of fear that they might otherwise disappear, but out of delight that we have been granted this relational foretaste of heaven.

Some of my favorite people in the world are people I rarely see or communicate with. If I had unlimited time and unlimited money, I could happily spend every waking hour for the rest of my life texting and emailing and visiting them all. But alas, I'm a finite human with other demands on my time and money. (As are they, in almost every case.) Our reunions never feel long enough or frequent enough.

Still, I count myself privileged to know and love an inconvenient number of people. It would take me an eternity to spend all the time I wish I could spend with every one of them.

Thank goodness I'll have an eternity at my disposal.

10

Friendship Costs Twenty-Five Dollars an Hour

Notes from an Alien Anthropologist:
The human creatures are quick to ask the question, "Who can I belong with?" They are much slower to ask, "Who can belong with me?" With demand far outstripping supply, the human struggle to belong appears to be an economic inevitability.

The same year I started grad school at Penn State, I also picked up a side job as a GRE tutor. (The GRE—short for "Graduate Record Exam"—is an entrance exam for grad school, kind of like a more advanced SAT or ACT.) When my supervisor at the tutoring agency wrote to introduce me to my first client, there was a single sentence of ominous warning: "I get the sense that he's a bit . . . eccentric."

Buck, age thirty-six, had a shaved head, a round face, and the fast-talking twang of a rural car salesman. When I called to introduce myself and arrange our first meeting, Buck insisted that we hold our tutoring sessions in his apartment.

"That's against my company's policy," I told him apologetically. "I'm only permitted to meet in a public place, like a library or an office."

"No, you see," said Buck, "this *is* my office. I have a home office. It's not like you'd be coming into my bedroom or anything. It's very professional. So you wouldn't be breaking any rules."

"I suppose I can run it by my supervisor," I said.

"I don't see why you'd need to run it by anyone," he said, and then repeated: "You wouldn't be breaking any rules."

I sent an email to my supervisor, who gave me license to meet anywhere that would keep Buck happy. And then another line, a harbinger of things to come: "He's such an odd duck."

Buck's apartment was on the seventh floor of a red brick tower in the heart of downtown State College. He ushered me through an expensive but unkempt living room, high-end electronics and pristine furniture covered in a detritus of half-emptied snack boxes and bits of clothing. "Sorry about all this mess," he said. "It's my girlfriend. Women, you know? She's from the Ukraine. Her English isn't the greatest. But you don't need to talk for the important stuff, you know?"

I didn't know. I said nothing.

"And this is my office," he said, leading the way in. "No women in here. But still messy, you know? Look at that view. Best view in State College."

"Gorgeous," I agreed, looking out past the roofs of the sur- rounding buildings to the rolling green hills at the edge of town and the wooded slope of Mount Nittany.

"They told me there was nothing available on the seventh floor. Wanted to rent me some piece of trash apartment on the second floor. All you can see from the balcony down there is traffic. That's not a view. But I didn't back down. I made sure they knew who had the money, you know? And before you know it, they're saying they've got an open apartment on the seventh floor. After what I told them, they wouldn't dare offer it to anybody else. And here we are. That's how you do it, buddy."

His laugh was all in the nose, three short bursts of percussion. An aggressive laugh. The kind of laugh that seemed to demand everyone else laugh along.

I didn't laugh.

"Let's talk about the GRE," I said. And our first session began.

○ ○ ○

For a man paying me by the hour, Buck had remarkably little interest in the GRE. He was constantly interrupting our sessions to tell stories, and then interrupting those stories with other stories: "I'm not too worried about the GRE essays, because I've got lots of experience with writing. When I was in prison—oh, look at your face, you didn't know I'd been in prison! Yeah, I got mixed up in some bad stuff, tax stuff, but it wasn't really my fault, actually; I was set up by my business partner, what a jagoff. But I wrote a book while I was in prison, and then I got out early because of good behavior. I'm not on parole anymore, now that I'm out of rehab from the drugs. Because there was the drugs, too, and the tax stuff. And that's why I'm going to school later in life. It's not because I'm slow in the head or anything. Actually, I'm kind of a genius. Mensa invited me to join, but I don't want to waste all that money on dues, you know? One time I took this IQ test . . ."

The longer Buck talked, the more skeptical I became. Was he really a well-respected martial artist? Was he really on track to singlehandedly take down the Church of Scientology in court? Was his undergraduate work in economics really being published in prestigious journals and transforming the way the United States thought about money?

Google confirmed that he was an ex-Scientologist with a drug history and a rich father. Beyond that, I only had his word.

His *words*, rather. There were a lot of them.

"I think my GRE client might be a pathological liar," I told a friend. "Or a bizarrely accomplished ex-con. Or maybe he's just unhinged."

"Scary," my friend answered.

"I don't know," I said. "He seems harmless enough. I think he just likes having someone to lie to."

Not long after that, Buck told me he wanted to hire me for additional tutoring hours. "But we'll do it off the books. I'll pay you directly, instead of through the tutoring agency. You'll make more money that way, and it won't cost me as much."

"I don't think that's legal," I said. "But I can check with my supervisor."

"Of course it's legal," he said. "No sense wasting everyone's time by asking. You wouldn't be breaking any rules."

"Still," I said, "let me just check with my supervisor."

"I already got his permission," said Buck. "He says it's fine."

I talked with my supervisor. It wasn't fine.

"They're being so unreasonable," Buck told me when I returned for our next session. "I'm not made of money. Would you like a cigarette? Mind if I have one?"

○ ○ ○

Buck's girlfriend, Ulyana, was out of the apartment for our first few sessions. As the autumn wore on, though, I saw her more and more often. She might be watching TV as I came in, or she would poke her head into the office mid-session to tell Buck she was going grocery shopping. Once when I arrived at the apartment, she answered the front door in her pajamas, inviting me inside with her unmistakable Ukrainian accent: "Buck is not yet home. You will wait in office?"

Buck showed up ten or fifteen minutes later, thoroughly apologetic. "I forgot you were coming today, which is why I'm late, and Ulyana wasn't really dressed. But I mean, in those pajamas, she just . . . you know what I mean?"

I didn't know, but it seemed best not to dwell on it.

Halfway through that session, Buck looked up from the sentence completion exercises we were studying and yelled into the next room, "Ulyana! Can you bring us a snack?"

"Get it yourself!" she yelled back.

"We're working right now!" he yelled. "Greg's on the clock! And he's hungry!"

Buck turned to me, lowering his voice. "You're hungry, right?"

A few minutes later, Ulyana brought us a plateful of Ritz crackers spread with cream cheese and topped with smoked salmon. She shot Buck a reproachful look before turning politely to me. "You would like some tea?"

It seemed rude not to accept. Buck's smile widened. "Have a cracker too," he said. "They're delicious. Ulyana makes them so perfect."

When the tutoring session ended and my mug was still half full, Buck insisted I take my tea to go, and Ulyana transferred it into a red Solo cup. Which is why I stepped onto the downtown streets of a college town at 5:00 p.m. on a Friday carrying a red Solo cup full of brown liquid, taking sips as I walked, looking for all the world like a college student in search of a good time and in flagrant violation of Pennsylvania's open container laws.

From the lawns of the frat houses I passed, shirtless fraternity brothers nodded admiringly at my beverage boldness. I nodded back without disabusing them of their assumptions. It's not every day a tea-drinking, GRE-tutoring grad student gets noticed by the cool kids.

○ ○ ○

Over time, Buck and Ulyana seemed to forget that I was a professional acquaintance. I had become, in their minds, something more like a salaried friend. I was in their apartment twice a week, after all. Ulyana had grown accustomed to bringing me snacks and mugs of tea. Buck was telling me intimate details from his past, casting visions of his dreams and aspirations for the future. "Once I'm the CEO of my own business," he said, "I'm going to hire you. It'll pay so much more than this tutoring thing, more than you'd ever make as an English professor. Because we work well together, you and

me. You're such a smart guy. Such a good guy. That's why I've got
to hire you."

"But first," I said, pointing at the book, "you've got to find the
volume of this rectangular prism."

For my part, I was a bit uncomfortable with the nontutoring
parts of our relationship. But I was too conflict avoidant—too
Indonesian—to do anything other than play along. Besides, why
wouldn't I want to get paid to eat finger food and swap stories with
the strangest man I had ever met?

I tracked the progress of my relationship with Buck by the meta-
morphosis of his email signatures. Early in the fall semester, he
signed all his emails to me with two unpunctuated lines:

Your student
Buck

Around Thanksgiving, he upgraded to this:

Your friend
Your student
Buck

And finally, just in case the new signature had seemed too pre-
sumptuous, he added a third line of digital genuflecting:

Most humbly
Your friend
Your student
Buck

Whatever humility Buck had in his email signatures, he didn't
seem to feel the need to express it in person. His stories had only
grown more self-aggrandizing as the months passed. Chances were
good, it seemed, that Buck would be getting into politics soon.
People liked him, and he knew how to *actually* make the system
work. All things considered, he'd make a pretty excellent president

of the United States. (It seemed I would be his campaign manager. Or his speechwriter. Or something like that.)

Jesus came up every once in a while in our conversations. Buck wasn't what you'd call a conventionally religious person. But he was, he informed me, "really spiritual." After a disastrous breakup with Scientology, Buck had decided that he was more-or-less Christian. "I don't want to be in church or anything like that," he said. "Christians get a lot of stuff wrong. Spirituality, for me, it's more about making peace with all the parts of yourself. That's what Jesus was all about. I wrote about it in my book—you know, the one I wrote in prison."

I expressed the requisite level of interest in his book and agreed that Jesus does indeed bring peace to his followers. "But it seems to me," I said, "that if we really take seriously the claims that Jesus made about himself, we can't stop there. If Jesus is telling the truth, then shouldn't the truth he tells radically re-order our lives?"

"Well," said Buck. He seemed a bit taken aback that I was being so contrarian. "We can't all be as holy as you. But maybe if I pray, Jesus will give me a good score on the GRE." And back to work we went.

The emails kept coming, every one reminding me of how intimate our relationship had ostensibly become:

Most humbly
Your friend
Your student
Buck

Friend certainly wasn't the word I would have chosen to describe Buck. I still didn't trust him as far as I could throw his ergonomically correct office chair. I still thought he was entitled and sexist and astoundingly amoral. I still hated the way my shirts reeked of cigarette smoke when I left his apartment.

And yet . . . we weren't quite non-friends, either.

I spent time with him (at the highly affordable rate of twenty-five dollars an hour). I cared about him. I hoped good things for him. I almost even liked him a little bit.

We took a break from tutoring for Christmas. Buck assured me that he was eager to finish conquering the GRE come springtime. His email's exact words were, "WE'LL DO A GREAT JOB!!!!!"

We. I was sharing pronouns with him now.

Pretty intimate stuff.

○ ○ ○

When spring came, all I heard was crickets. I ran into Buck on campus one day, and he greeted me with an enthusiastic hug. "I put the GRE on hold. I'm taking a gap year to focus on developing my business. I'm gonna get in touch with you about working with us. It's just so great to see you."

"Likewise," I said. The jury was out on whether I was being polite or sincere.

We parted ways for the last time. Three full months of spring came and went, and I almost forgot that Buck existed.

In May, once I'd assigned final grades to my undergraduate students and submitted final papers to my graduate professors, I drove up to my grandmother's house in Pleasantville to spend the week. I was browsing Facebook from her living room couch when an article posted by a friend caught my eye. A man from State College, thirty-six years old, had fallen to his death from a seventh floor balcony.

"I've been in this apartment building before," my friend wrote on Facebook.

I looked at the picture more closely. I, too, had been in that apartment building. On the seventh floor. With a thirty-six-year-old man.

The following day, police released his name. The investigation was ongoing, but everyone suspected suicide.

There was a phone number I was supposed to call if I had any information related to Buck's death. I had plenty of information, but nothing the police wanted to know. I knew which kinds of math problems gave him the most trouble. I knew that when he wrote essays, he had a habit of capitalizing random Nouns in the middle of his Sentences, like he was Emily Dickinson reincarnate. I knew (to my chagrin) which of Ulyana's physical features he found most attractive. I knew he could smile and tell me how happy he was in one moment, and then be filled with blind rage at the world the next moment. I knew he wasn't as happy as his persona demanded that he pretend to be.

Buck had told me a lot of lies, but perhaps his happiness had been the biggest lie of all.

I went to the kitchen to get a glass of water. Grandma was there, chopping vegetables for dinner. I offered to help, but she graciously declined.

"I just read about one of my former students in the news," I said. "He committed suicide."

She stopped chopping. "Oh, how awful," she said, sounding quintessentially grandmotherly. "Did you know him well?"

"No," I said. "Apparently not."

○ ○ ○

I never thought of myself as belonging with Buck. As far as I was concerned, all my belonging was happening with other people—people who were easier to love, and who weren't paying me by the hour. I felt about Buck the way I felt about nuts in my brownies: fine when I was in the mood, but also a low-key nuisance.

It wasn't until after he died that I began to wonder whether Buck had felt like he belonged with me.

When I first moved to Pennsylvania, I had prayed, "God, help me find people with whom I can belong here." That prayer had been thoroughly answered. But I had forgotten, like the perpetual narcissist I am, to pray the other side of the prayer: "God, help me find people to whom I can give the gift of belonging."

We all want to receive self-sacrificial love from others. We all want to be accepted and welcomed and taken in, even and especially when we're at our very worst. But almost nobody wants to do the accepting and welcoming and taking in. Almost nobody wants to go around finding the most unpleasant, most undeserving people available and declaring, *I choose you. You belong with me now.*

It never occurred to me to make intentional space in my heart for Buck. He was the textbook definition of a Bad Influence, the kind of guy whose ethics were so sparse you could see the tumbleweed rolling through. It would have been easier to attend a vegetarians' conference in a hot dog costume than to bring Buck along to parties and take responsibility for his unsavory sense of humor: "That guy who just made the chauvinist joke? He's my, um, friend . . ."

Would Jesus have chosen to belong with Buck?

I'm not suggesting that this question has a single self-evident answer. Jesus was no pushover, after all. He set relational boundaries for himself, and some people chose not to be around him on the basis of those boundaries. He repulsed by his very nature the murderers who wanted to keep on murdering, the liars who wanted to keep on lying, the hypocrites who wanted to keep on hypocrite-ing.

Jesus also had tiers of friendship. He distinguished between close friends and slightly-less-close friends—even among the twelve disciples, John got a lot more affection than Thaddaeus. Jesus loved humankind without limits, but not every person in every crowd received equal attention from him.

Still, behind all these caveats, I can't escape the feeling that I missed something when it came to Buck. Maybe I don't need to know exactly *what* I missed in order to know that I missed it. Maybe I don't need an answer to the question so much as I need the question itself: *Would Jesus have chosen to belong with Buck?*

This much I do know: If we only ever pay attention to our own sense of belonging, without giving a second thought to the belonging of others, we might miss out on the moments when our location in the world matters most. Those who belong like Jesus belonged don't just *receive* the gift of belonging; we turn around and give it away.

Of course, maybe Buck's increasingly intimate email signatures, the food he offered and the stories he told, were all just part of the persona he was playing. Maybe the friendship he said he felt toward me was just another lie I had fallen for.

A voice on one shoulder whispers in my ear, *You barely even knew him. Half of what he told you was probably fake. Why should he matter to you?*

To which the voice on the other shoulder replies, *Why shouldn't he?*

The Origami Artists

Notes from an Alien Anthropologist:
The human word family *is really two different words, spelled and pronounced the same, often confused with one another. Many of the human creatures think they need one kind of family to be happy, when in fact it's the other kind of family they're searching for.*

I'm not what you'd call "good with kids." I once tried to entertain a six-month-old child by telling him the meaning of the word *defenestration*. "Isn't it delightful, James," I said, bouncing the infant up and down in my arms, "that the English language has given us a single word to describe the act of throwing someone or something out a window? D-E-F-E-N-E-S-T-R-A-T-I-O-N."

James, unfortunately, did not share my enthusiasm. He promptly started crying, and his mother rushed over to rescue him from my seminar.

Lots of adults seem to have a switch installed in their brains, flipping like a circuit breaker every time a child approaches. The pitch of their voice rises, their vocabulary level plummets, and they develop an inexplicable fascination with crayons and fire trucks. They don't even need a phone booth to perform their split-second wardrobe change from regular-adult-Clark-Kent to kindergarten-teacher-Superman.

Here's what happens to me when I encounter a child:

Absolutely nothing.

I have no switch installed. I talk in the same tone and use the same words I would use with my grad school professors. I don't have a separate personality or set of interests stored away for my younger acquaintances, to be pulled out like plastic dishes and Disney-themed napkins when company comes over.

In my world, everybody gets the same napkins.

Let me hasten to say, it's not that I don't *like* kids. On the contrary, when I meet a child who wants to have a real human conversation with me, a child who can tolerate polysyllabic words and grown-up napkins, I'm thoroughly delighted. I've simply given up on trying to appeal to children (or adults, for that matter) who expect me to behave in ways I'm not gifted to behave.

When I was in middle school and high school, my brother John and I would often be tasked, alongside our friends Sarah and Hannah, with the job of looking after the younger kids during our parents' work meetings. John and Hannah were the ones good with kids, the ones clearly destined to become exemplary parents. Their touch could soothe the most colicky of infants. Toddlers and elementary-age children flocked to them, played endless silly games with them, and adored them.

Sarah and I tried to help, but more often than not we wound up in a corner somewhere, keeping an eye on one or two stray youngsters while we talked about literature. The children did not flock to us. "If we ever have kids," we told each other fatalistically, "they're going to love their Uncle John and Aunt Hannah way more than they love us."

When I reported this conversation to my mom, she reassured me that she had often felt the same way. "I babysat exactly once when I was in high school," she said. "It was awful. I don't naturally enjoy hanging out with other people's kids. But when I had my own kids, it was different. If you and Sarah have your own kids, it'll be different."

Sarah did have her own kids years later, beating both Hannah and John to the natal punch. Sure enough, she was (and is) a terrific mother. John and Hannah are terrific parents too, though this surprises no one.

As for me, I said a tentative goodbye to the idea of having kids in the same moment I concluded I was probably going to be single and celibate for my entire life. I told myself it was fitting for someone so obviously ill-suited to childcare to remain childless. Sometimes I even felt relieved. Greg-Without-Kids would not be woken up in the night for weeks and months on end to take care of a wailing baby. Greg-Without-Kids was mostly exempt from dealing with other people's poop and urine and vomit and blood. Greg-Without-Kids would have so much more time to invest in other pursuits, pursuits I was more gifted in and more passionate about.

But sometimes, Greg-Without-Kids didn't want to be passionate about things in solitude. Sometimes I dreamed of sharing my life's ordinary moments with mini-humans who might adopt my fascinations and mimic my mannerisms—who might grow up differently because they had grown up in my company.

Sometimes the thought of never having kids felt like a tremendous loss. Sometimes it still does.

○ ○ ○

I became friends with Grant and Max Henning because of Grant's adenoids. It might have happened anyway, eventually, by some other means. But in our case, the adenoids get the credit.

Before the adenoids, Grant and Max and I interacted mostly at a cordial distance. Their dad, Aaron, was the lead pastor of my church in State College, where I started attending as a twenty-three-year-old grad student. Their mom, Amy, sometimes sang on worship teams with me. But Grant was six years old, and Max was three, and I was—as we've already established—no virtuoso with kids that age. "Delightful to see you, gentlemen," I would say to the boys, offering them fist bumps while I chatted with their parents.

They returned my fist bumps shyly. "Hello," Grant would say, polite but skeptical, while Max studied me with large curious eyes.

Right around his seventh birthday, Grant was scheduled for surgery to have his adenoids removed. I wasn't sure what adenoids were, exactly, or what they contributed to the body. As far as I could tell from a brief Google search, they were kind of like the appendix: a body part that exists solely for the purpose of being surgically removed every once in a while.

Our mutual friend Jill, an elementary gym teacher who is as brilliant with kids as I am awkward, suggested to Grant that the two of them throw a party after the surgery. "We'll call it the After-Adenoid Party," said Jill. "It's gonna be a dance party. You've got to bring all your best dance moves. When people hear how cool our After-Adenoid Party is, they'll all wish they were getting their adenoids removed too."

I never did figure out how I ended up on the guest list for the After-Adenoid Party. Maybe being friends with Jill made me cool by association. Maybe Aaron and Amy used their parental influence to convince Grant that he liked all the same people they did. Or maybe Grant was simply one of those rare children who appreciated my refusal to treat seven-year-olds differently than I treated adults.

Whatever the reason, Jill and I wound up in the Hennings' kitchen on a Friday night to celebrate Grant's successful adenoidectomy. Jill and Grant danced boisterously around the kitchen after dinner, just as promised. Max and I abstained, watching the dancers from our chairs while Aaron and Amy scooped leftovers into Tupperware. "They look hilarious, don't they?" I said to Max. He nodded, studying us all with his large curious eyes.

The After-Adenoid Party became the pilot episode for a series of future evenings Jill and I would spend with the Hennings. We called the series Fun Fridays, although sometimes we branched out to other days of the week: Wacky Wednesdays, Thrilling Thursdays, Superb Saturdays. There were never as many Fun Fridays as anyone wanted, but like the BBC's *Sherlock* series, our episodes made up in quality what they lacked in quantity.

In the precious moments before dinner, and then again between dessert and the boys' bedtime, Grant and Max and I became friends. They would perform their latest piano pieces for me, or offer me a guided tour of their latest LEGO creations, or teach me to fly their remote-controlled helicopter through the hazardous skies of the living room. One evening shortly after Grant's ninth birthday, we were all eating Blizzards at Dairy Queen when I mentioned that I had recently learned the scientific name for an ice cream headache: *sphenopalatine ganglioneuralgia.*

"What was that again?" said Grant, setting down his spoon and pulling a pen out of his pocket. Grant was the sort of nine-year-old who traveled with pens in his pocket. "Can you spell it for me?"

He scrawled the words on a napkin and spent the rest of the evening practicing them. The following Sunday at church, when I asked five-year-old Max how his morning was going, he answered triumphantly: "Pretty good, because I don't have sphenopalatine ganglioneuralgia."

"Can you give us another word?" said Grant, approaching with a scrap of green paper and a poised pen.

"How about floccinaucinihilipilification?" I said.

"Perfect," said Grant matter-of-factly, as Max's eyes widened. "How do you spell that?"

○ ○ ○

I am not, in the physiological sense of the word, a eunuch. And yet, based on the amount of sex I'm currently having and the number of biological offspring I expect to leave behind when I die, the distinction between me and a eunuch sometimes feels negligible.

I am, as far as I can tell, precisely the kind of person Jesus has in view when he says in Matthew 19, "There are eunuchs who were born that way, and there are eunuchs who have been made eunuchs by others—and there are those who choose to live like eunuchs for the sake of the kingdom of heaven." I seem to fit that third category rather well: the people who live a sexless and childless life, not because they have no other options, but because they truly believe that the kingdom of heaven is worth every ounce of their devotion.

For people of Jesus' day, one of the great tragedies of a eunuch's life was that he would never have the opportunity to become a biological parent. His bloodline would end the day he died, leaving no one behind to carry on his legacy or to prove that his time on earth had mattered. Infertile women of that era faced the same fear. So did every married couple unable to conceive children together for any reason. To be without offspring was to go unremembered.

Perhaps it's fitting that Jesus' next act in Matthew 19—just after describing people who, like Jesus himself, live as eunuchs by choice—is to place his hands on and pray for the little children who are brought to him. He doesn't withdraw from the lives of children simply because he's not the one parenting them. On the contrary, Jesus declares children central to the kingdom of heaven. He invests in them, takes them seriously, invites them to follow in his footsteps of passionate love for God and neighbor.

For Jesus' disciples, biological parenting isn't meant to be the only way we leave a legacy or build a family. It's not even meant to be the *primary* way we leave a legacy or build a family. Jesus treats the family of God as something much more substantial than just a pretty metaphor. It is a concrete claim, a literal state of being. Those who follow God together are family to one another.

At the end of Matthew 19, Jesus promises that the people who give up the usual trappings of home and spouse and children for the sake of the gospel will receive a hundred times as much in return. In short, he is promising us the family of God. He is promising us to one another. If this promise doesn't sound like good news—if the family of God sounds like a cheap substitute for a spouse and a picket fence and two-and-a-quarter children—perhaps it's because we in the church have failed to really live like family to one another.

Do we believe that nuclear family is in some way superior—more permanent, more dependable, more meaningful, more concrete—than spiritual family? Jesus certainly didn't seem to. Maybe it's time for those of us who claim to follow him to step up our game and start acting like actual sisters and brothers and fathers and mothers to one another. Maybe we need to start being for one another the family Jesus promised we would be for one another.

Another of my favorite biblical promises for single people comes from the book of Isaiah:

> And let no eunuch complain,
>   "I am only a dry tree."

For this is what the LORD says:

> "To the eunuchs who keep my Sabbaths,
>   who choose what pleases me
>   and hold fast to my covenant—
> to them I will give within my temple and
>   its walls
>   a memorial and a name
>   better than sons and daughters;
> I will give them an everlasting name
>   that will endure forever." (56:3-5)

I'm not saying that those of us who remain single, or those couples unable to conceive biological kids, can't still become parents. Fostering and adoption are beautiful and necessary modes of parenting that are open to us all—even the celibates. My point is, rather, that every follower of Jesus is called to leave a legacy, to partake in the family of God, to participate in the lives of those younger than us, regardless of whether we ever become parents in a biological or legal sense.

There is something we lose when our obedience to Jesus leaves us childless. But if Jesus is telling the truth, we gain much more than we could possibly lose.

○ ○ ○

"Max and I can't decide if you're more like a brother or a weird uncle," Grant told me at dinner one evening.

"Uncle Greg doesn't sound quite right," Max chimed in. "But you'd be a really old older brother."

"Jill's definitely an aunt," Grant declared. "But Greg, I don't know. Greg could be a little bit of both."

Whatever the nature of my relationship with Grant and Max, I don't have a name for it either. All I know is that the part of my heart they've taken up residence in is a part I didn't know existed before I met them. I've watched them grow taller across six years of hugs, from the days when Max's arms still wrapped around my legs to the moment Grant's tousled hair could tickle the underside of my chin. I've watched them lose teeth and regain teeth, witnessed their first pairs of glasses, and affixed their ever-changing school pictures to my fridge door with magnets. I've watched their personalities mature, seen them become more thoroughly themselves.

And once in a while, by some outrageous unearned privilege, I've seen traces of evidence that my brother-uncle presence in their lives has mattered.

Grant has been known to lecture people on the pluralization of neuter nouns in ancient Greek, explaining why the preferred plural of the English word *phenomenon* is *phenomena* rather than *phenomenons*. "When people say I'm weird," Grant tells me, "I take it as a compliment." Our mutual friends will sometimes come to me shaking their heads after a conversation with Grant and murmur, "It's obvious the two of you hang out a lot."

Max can tell you the difference between *sanguine* (meaning cheerfully optimistic) and *sanguinary* (meaning bloodthirsty), and he knows about the ancient medical theory of the four humors that caused these two words to share a common root. For a period of several months, I would greet him by asking whether he was feeling more sanguine or sanguinary that day. "Sanguinary!" he would declare, then lunge at me with bared teeth and pretend to bite my arm.

The boys went through a season where they were both obsessed with origami. (I, too, had such a season in my own childhood.) The three of us would fold together sometimes, once begging Aaron and Amy to push back bedtime by five or ten minutes so we could finish a complex three-dimensional design we were right in the middle of. For almost a year, the boys would give me origami creations every time we were together. As the months wore on, my apartment filled up with handmade paper gifts, so many I lost count.

"Do you remember a time before we knew Greg?" Amy once asked the origami artists.

"A little bit," said Grant, squinting hard. "But not really."

"I don't," said Max definitively. "Greg's always been part of the family."

There's no way of knowing for certain what our friendship will look like in future years. Perhaps as the boys grow into teenagerhood and adulthood, they'll stop calling me Crookshanks, and perhaps they'll grow tired of hearing me call them Groozlenut and Swellmack. But every minute I spend with them, every fond hug and fist bump, feels like proof that Jesus told the truth. Proof that the unearned and undeserved family God gives his disciples can still be better than any other family we might have tried to eke out for ourselves.

My moments with Grant and Max pile up like origami gifts, imperfect and unassuming and breathtakingly beautiful.

12

Laundering

Notes from an Alien Anthropologist:
The human creatures are addicted to the spectacular, seeking fulfillment in it, even though the deepest longings of their soul are either met or left unmet, not in the spectacular, but in the ordinary day-to-day.

For the last seven years, I've driven a beige Mercury Montego named The Retirement Vehicle. I call him that both because he looks like one and because I'd be thrilled if he lasted me that long. He has all the amenities you could want in a retirement vehicle: heated seats, a spacious trunk, a moonroof, an analog clock, and a six-CD player mostly populated by CDs I owned in high school.

Had I been placed in charge of crafting a car for myself, the fruit of my imagination would have been nothing like The Retirement Vehicle. But I don't love him any less as a result. If anything, I most savor the bits of him I wouldn't have picked for myself out of a catalog. I love his unnecessary amenities and his wide hips that fill out every parking space he squeezes into. I love the way I've never been pulled over while driving him, perhaps because the cops are pleasantly impressed to see a man of my advanced age speeding with the vigor of youth. Sometimes The Retirement Vehicle feels embarrassed about his lack of athleticism, but I reassure him that I love him just the way he is—his gentle acceleration and mediocre gas mileage and shallow turning radius notwithstanding. I wouldn't want him to be ostentatious and showy, even if he could be. I'm grateful that he is simple, familiar, ordinary.

In The Retirement Vehicle's front console, right next to a coin organizer that holds my quarters and nickels and dimes in neat stacks, I keep a garage door opener. The garage belongs to my friends Ben and Bethanne, who first gave me the garage door opener so I could keep an eye on their dog one weekend while they were out of town. I offered to return it to Ben the next time I saw him, but he declined. "You'll need to get into our house again," he said, in a tone of voice that could have indicated either a promise or a threat.

Knowing Ben, probably a bit of both.

As in the case of The Retirement Vehicle, I would never have thought to invent friends like Ben and Bethanne for myself. Ben is an Ivy League–educated law professor with a personal vendetta against exclamation points. Bethanne is an internationally acclaimed concert pianist turned stay-at-home mom, full to bursting with all the social graces her husband scrupulously avoids. The names of their three children are taken from people and places in J. R. R. Tolkien's *Lord of the Rings*.

We met at church, where Amy and I immediately began courting Bethanne as a prospective worship team member. (I was charged with "auditioning" her, though the thought of me passing judgment on her piano aptitude was laughable.) Only later did we discover that Ben knew his way around a guitar and had a warm tenor voice. Since one parent always needed to be at home with their *Lord of the Rings*–themed children, they joined the worship team on alternating weeks, Ben often playing guitar the same weeks I was scheduled for piano.

After rehearsal one Tuesday evening, Ben and I realized neither of us had eaten dinner yet. He invited me to join him for a late meal at Chick-fil-A. "I don't know," I said, glancing at the clock. "Chick-fil-A is on the other side of town."

"We live in State College," said Ben. "There are no sides of town."

His logic was irrefutable, as one would expect from a law professor. We went to Chick-fil-A. He insisted on paying for my dinner with a second irrefutable argument: "You're a grad student. And in the humanities, no less."

"Ouch," I said.

o o o

I've never known anyone to trample on ritual politeness more gleefully than Ben. "I have no empathy," he told me once. "I'm like a borderline sociopath who loves Jesus." One evening during an Advent service, upon hearing that we were about to "enjoy some music from the children's choir," Ben turned to me and said under his breath, "*Enjoy* is such a relative term." Another Sunday after church, Ben told me he and Bethanne were hosting a party that afternoon to celebrate their oldest daughter's sixth birthday. "I would invite you," he said, "but I like you."

Bethanne, by contrast, was polite and empathetic enough for the whole family of five. Her prolific mind could anticipate every possible source of offense and apologize for it in advance. "Ben doesn't really mean that," she would reassure me after her husband's bolder jokes, even if I was already laughing. When I accidentally lingered at their house after a holiday party until almost midnight, caught up in conversation with the two of them and Ben's mom, Robin, Bethanne apologized so profusely for keeping me that you would have thought she had barred the door and handcuffed me to the credenza.

It could have been either one of them who first offered to let me do laundry at their house. Bethanne was thoughtful enough to think of such things, and Ben was brazen enough to initiate them. For my part, I was enough of a mooch to accept the offer. I started showing up in their driveway with a mesh bag teeming with socks and undershirts slung over my shoulder, looking like the Santa Claus of dirty laundry. Robin helped me fold clean laundry one evening, handling my tartan boxers without flinching. "You're the right age to be one of my sons," she said matter-of-factly, "and I folded Benny's underpants for years."

Laundry became our rhythmic excuse for spending time together. If Ben or Bethanne wanted to hang out with me, they would say, "It's been a few weeks—don't you need to do laundry?" If I was running low on socks, I would say, "We should get together soon (on an evening your washer and dryer aren't otherwise occupied)." We didn't always spend time together while my laundry was in process; occasionally I would let myself in with the garage door opener when they were out of the house, or I would bring a backpack full of work and edit manuscript pages between machine cycles. But mostly we just sat around drinking water and talking, our tongues loosened by the knowledge that we were stuck with each other for at least an hour and a half.

"I hope it's not a hassle," I said one evening during the wash cycle, "feeling like you have to put your life on hold and chat with me whenever I need clean underwear."

"Of *course* not," Bethanne effused. "I love it. It's like drinking a hot beverage with a friend: you can't drink it fast without burning your tongue, so you might as well slow down and talk for a long time. It's forced lingering."

When people ask me what genuine hospitality looks like, a few images spring readily into my mind, and my laundering with Ben and Bethanne is one of them. Though the two of them can be marvelous hosts when the occasion demands, the traditional "hosting" elements are usually absent from our laundry evenings. I let myself in the door, and Ben hollers a greeting from the living room without bothering to come downstairs. I head directly to the laundry room, then help myself to a glass of water from the kitchen and refill the water pitcher if it's getting low. Bethanne eventually extricates herself from the children long enough to give me a hug and apologize for all the toys on the floor. "Do you need dinner?" she asks. "I didn't think it was very good, but there's still a bunch on the stove."

Hospitality doesn't wait for perfection. It doesn't demand that the kids be incarcerated in their bedrooms and the floors purged of princess paraphernalia. Hospitality welcomes us into life as it is, on tidy days and chaotic ones alike, offering the food that's there without worrying whether it's a gourmet feast. Hospitality is simple, familiar, ordinary.

Hospitality risks being unimpressive in order to be present.

Perhaps *unimpressive* is the wrong word to describe Ben and Bethanne, the Ivy League–educated law professor and the internationally acclaimed concert pianist. But the more they become people with whom I belong—not just people who occasionally squeeze me into their social calendar, but people who own the machines where I do all my laundering—the more their impressiveness subsides to make way for their humanity. They feel less like a fireworks show and more like a sunrise: a spectacle of light that lingers again and again, willingly compelled into repetition, joining the rhythm of my world.

o o o

On summer evenings after sunset, I often walk in silence around my neighborhood, following in reverse the same five-kilometer route Ben and I use for our morning jogs. For an hour or so, my feet have a job to do, but my mind has no scheduled commitments. I listen to the cicadas, watch fireflies sparkle like out-of-season Christmas lights among the oak trees. I talk to God, leaving enough space for him to talk back if he has something to say. I strip down the engine of my soul until nothing is left but stillness and being and listening.

Forced lingering, Bethanne would say. Me and my Creator, joyfully constrained to linger together.

The people we linger with are the people we grow to love. There is no deep belonging without deep lingering.

Sometimes when I get home from the walk, I'm still not done lingering. I take a detour to the parking lot and sit on The Retirement Vehicle's ample trunk, lying back against his sloping rear windshield and staring up at faint gray clouds as they drift past the moon. I breathe in summer night air. The wind blows gently around me, as if God is breathing too, lingering with me.

13

Ghosts of Friendship Past

Notes from an Alien Anthropologist:
The human creatures are determined to shield themselves from the pain of heartache. But a heart shielded from heartache is equally shielded from beauty.

We met for coffee at the Starbucks in Barnes & Noble. I was seated first, burning my upper lip with impatient sips of hot apple cider, tensing and untensing my abdomen in an effort to unknit the knot in my stomach.

"I'll get a drink before we start," he said when he arrived, leaving a thick leather Bible on the table across from me.

For a few minutes, I stared at the Bible, wondering which of its words he planned to read to me. Wondering what those words and their interpretation(s) would mean for my life, for his, for our church.

Tensing. Untensing. Tensing. Untensing. The apple cider was still too hot to drink.

He returned with a coffee cup, sat down, and began the gracious preliminaries. He told me how much he and his wife loved me, how much his kids enjoyed my friendship, how much the whole family delighted to be led by me in worship. He told me what an admirable young man I was.

When he reached for the Bible, I knew the preamble was over.

○ ○ ○

Roughly one year prior, my pastor Aaron and I had been standing in the Henning family driveway, talking about my plans to publicly come out as gay and celibate in a forthcoming book. Aaron was in the middle of a home improvement project, brushing shellac onto a long pine board while I stood uselessly by, as if to illustrate how well the two of us fit our respective stereotypes as a straight man and a not-so-straight one.

"Do you think people are going to leave the church because of me?" I asked.

"I'd like to think they won't." He hesitated. "But probably."

My eyes followed the rhythm of his brush, the shimmer of the fresh resin. "Would it be easier for people to handle if I wasn't leading worship?"

"Maybe," he said. "But I don't want you to stop leading worship."

"I don't want to wreck the church," I said.

He stopped shellacking long enough to look me in the eye. "Three years ago, when we were praying for a worship leader and you showed up, I believed God had brought you to our church for a reason. I still believe that. No matter what happens, the Hennings are with you."

○ ○ ○

I had imagined the conversation in the Barnes & Noble Starbucks (or something like it) a hundred times before. I had imagined meeting with a concerned congregant or two, trying to assuage their concerns and defend my orthodoxy, not knowing if they'd still want to share a church with me when the conversation was over. But my imagination was so much different than the reality. The conversation I'd imagined was devoid of relationship, punctuated with yelling and literal Bible thumping. The person on the other side of the table had always been a faceless stranger, someone who could disappear from my life without leaving me feeling like an amputee.

I hadn't imagined a friend or a parent of friends. Not someone I liked and admired. Not someone I loved.

It never occurred to me that theological debate could feel so much like heartbreak.

Both of us spoke slowly. He, as if watering a plant, each sentence slowly dribbled onto my dry soil, waiting for the words to sink in before he continued. I, like a PhD student taking an oral exam, fearing every misplaced syllable would be fiercely scrutinized.

I won't drag you through the blow-by-blow of our argument, the nuanced differences in our anthropology and philology and hamartiology, the prolonged painful read aloud of the Sodom story in Genesis 18 and 19 to illustrate the inherent moral turpitude of same-sex orientation. (Suffice it to say that neither of us was converted by the other.)

We concluded in prayer. He prayed aloud as I sat in silence, head bowed and palms open, agreeing with at least 90 percent of what he said. When he stood up, I followed suit. We shook hands.

"I appreciate you having this conversation with me first," I said. "But it sounds like the next conversation you need to have is with our pastors. I do hope you and your family keep worshiping with us."

"Thanks for your time," he said.

He went out to the parking lot. I couldn't bear the thought of walking in step behind him, so I sat back down with my now-tepid apple cider. I took small cautious sips, as if it were still scalding, as if heat from an hour ago still had the power to burn me.

o o o

I had exactly one more face-to-face conversation with him and his wife. They were meeting with Aaron after church one Sunday, trying to determine how firmly our church's elders stood in support of me and what that support meant for their own church membership. I was in a room down the hall with Amy, prepping music sheets for next week's worship rehearsal.

It was only by accident that we made eye contact as they walked out of Aaron's office. But once we'd made eye contact, we all felt compelled to follow through with the pleasantries. They both gave me long, tight hugs. "We love you," said the wife tearfully.

"I love you guys too," I said.

She wasn't lying. Neither was I. And yet, somehow, I had the feeling we were both saying goodbye.

When I used to imagine what it would be like to have someone leave a church because of me, I thought it would be easy to forget them. I would be so angry at their rejection of me, so righteously indignant, that I would be relieved by their departure. "Good riddance!" I pictured myself declaring to their shrinking silhouettes, internally if not audibly. "Don't let the door hit you on the way out!" I was supposed to become immune to thinking of them, immune to missing them.

But the trouble with letting our lives become entangled with someone else's—the trouble with choosing to belong with someone—is that we can't just turn off affection like a spigot. Love leaks at inconvenient times, dribbling wasteful tears, no matter how much plumber's tape we wrap around it.

"Love anything," says C. S. Lewis in *The Four Loves*, "and your heart will be wrung and possibly broken." Love is risky because of our human tendency to go on loving even when it would be smarter to stop. Love is too persistent, too profligate, to be safe. When friendships die, their ghosts have a way of lingering.

Even after this couple left my church to worship elsewhere, we still lived in the same bit of rural Pennsylvania and ran in many of the same social circles. I was still friends with their kids, whom I saw regularly in bakeries and coffee shops, during Christian student events on the Penn State campus, even at church now and again. At potlucks I would sometimes find dishes labeled with their family name, helping myself to desserts prepared by a woman I had already said goodbye to for what I thought was the last time.

I saw ghosts even where there was nothing to see. Looking out from the piano on Sunday mornings, I saw them in the row of chairs their family used to fill. As I greeted newcomers at after-church luncheons, I saw the luncheon where I first met them, the one where I sat down at their table without invitation or introduction and insisted on memorizing all the children's names and ages.

I've heard people suggest that the only way to find closure from a broken relationship is to banish the ghosts forever. To stop caring. To treat the world as if no one who has wounded us—no one who has been wounded by us—ever existed in the first place.

But if our closure is only as strong as our forgetfulness, it's not really closure at all. Every meal we've shared, every song we've lip-synced while washing dishes, every church foyer and Barnes & Noble Starbucks where we've made memories together—all of it becomes a threat to our heart's fragile safety. When we banish the ghosts, we're forced to banish so much beauty along with them, until our world is just a fragile shell of its former self, always at risk of shattering.

I don't want to stop caring about the heartbreakers and the people whose hearts I've broken. I don't want to stop loving them or wish them out of existence. I just want to let go of the responsibility I used to feel to fix our relationship in this lifetime. I want to learn to say goodbye, to let our former intimacy drift into memory, without being afraid of the ghosts.

When I think of the people I've lost to conflict or failure or misunderstanding, I try to imagine us reuniting in heaven. I get excited for the perfected friendship we will enjoy, the perfect union we'll find in company with Jesus. I anticipate our every relational impediment being scrubbed away, every dispute finally answered and laid to rest, every wound healed.

Today we might be one another's heartbreakers. But when their hearts and mine are finally made whole, we won't call each other heartbreakers anymore. We'll simply be siblings and friends, fellow flesh in the consummate divine marriage.

In the meantime, I try to be grateful for the imperfect present. I pray that I'll keep on loving old friends, even if love feels out of season. Even if wisdom demands that we grow distant from one another for now. Even if nothing is ever restored until the final restoration of all things.

○ ○ ○

I was still sipping the same tepid apple cider at the Barnes & Noble Starbucks when a woman from my church walked past, pushing her one-year-old in a stroller. Hannah and her husband, Alex, were the sort of people I rarely spent time with but always enjoyed. For the first few years I knew them, Alex had identical wire-rim glasses and an identical blond buzzcut to mine. People confused us all the time, complimenting him on his piano playing, congratulating me on my lovely wife and newborn son. ("Thank you," I would tell them, "but Hannah's way out of my league.") In recognition of the trend, Alex and I called each other "doppelgänger."

"We're here to play with the trains," said my quasi-wife, radiating her usual effortless exuberance. "How are you?"

I almost lied, but something in her face persuaded me that she wanted the truth. "I've been better," I said.

She pulled the stroller out of the aisle, closer to the low metal railing that separated Starbucks from the bookshelves. "Do you need to talk about it? Milo and I have time."

There wasn't a lot I could tell her without feeling like I was violating some unspoken rule of confidentiality. There was even less I knew how to say without pressing into the tender bruises of the last hour-and-a-half. "It's complicated," I finally said. "I just finished a hard conversation. Someone might be leaving our church because of me."

"Because of . . . ?" She trailed off. "I'm sorry."

"Me too."

"I've been meaning to tell you," she said, as if changing the topic. "I just finished reading your book. It was beautiful. I'm so glad to know you and to have you in our church. And I would be proud if one of my kids grew up to be like you."

She might have said more, but I had stopped listening. I was crying—the ugly way, the noisy way, sucking air past a shivering lower lip to fill up my heaving chest.

"Can I give you a hug?" she said.

I accepted without words, reaching across the low railing and relaxing into her embrace. In the middle of Barnes & Noble, as rush-hour bibliophiles drifted past, she wrapped her arms around me as I shook and shook.

The Hennings volunteered to take me in for dinner that night. I cried again in the car on the way there, rolling down the windows to dry my face in the breeze. When I walked through the back door, Aaron was teaching seven-year-old Max the basics of algebra. Amy was at the stove, scraping vegetables from a cutting board into a wok. ("Are you okay?" she asked, her tone implying that if I *wasn't* okay, she would go put the fear of God in someone.) Ten-year-old Grant finished practicing piano and helped me set the table.

There was something blissful in the normalcy of it all. Neither of the boys seemed to notice my reddened eyes or the salty stiffness of my cheeks. We ate chicken stir-fry, reciting funny lines from movies and YouTube videos that Grant and Max had never watched but could still reproduce perfectly by mimicking their father.

The dining room was full of ghosts only I could see: Friendships that had already crumbled. Friendships I feared might crumble. Friendships mid-crumble, the cracks slowly lengthening before my eyes. Ghosts hunched under the tablecloth, clung to the ceiling fan, and refused to let me forget them. But heartbreak didn't feel so final when my world was teeming with hope.

I forget whether it was Max or Grant who, when I came through the door that evening and said I was staying for dinner, declared, "This is the best Monday ever." Somehow, despite everything, he was right.

14

Thank You for Making Me Hurt

Notes from an Alien Anthropologist:
As they say goodbye, many of the human creatures excrete saltwater from their eyes. The water appears to be a sign of momentary sadness, but also a sign of past and future happiness.

I never planned to stay in central Pennsylvania indefinitely. I moved to State College for grad school, which could only last so long before I finished my degree. (Or quit. Or exhausted my funding. Or flunked out.)

Everyone I met when I arrived understood that I was in State College in a grad student kind of way. Here by necessity, not by arbitrary preference. Here as long as necessary, and probably not much longer.

In academic settings, it was easy to remember that my days in State College were numbered. All my professional activity—my coursework, my research, my teaching—pointed toward the moment I would be out the door and beginning my first job as an English professor. My Penn State peers and professors and I all knew the job market for English professors was abysmal, but we still held out hope for the best. And in every best-case scenario, our calendars counted down to joyous departure. The longer I spent in grad school, the nearer its conclusion loomed.

Church, though, was a different story. The longer I spent in my church community—the longer I led worship and learned names and built friendships—the more people seemed to assume I would stay forever. "You don't *have* to graduate, do you?" my friend Andi would say, packing up her bass guitar after worship rehearsal. "If we sabotage your dissertation so you never finish your PhD, can we keep you?"

"I'd really rather finish the dissertation," I would tell her. "But if you sabotage me on the job market and no universities offer me a job, that should work just as well to keep me in town."

"We'll do that, then," she would nod, at which point her husband, Nate, would emerge from the drum cage to remind us both that he and Andi would love and support me no matter what, even if I accepted a job far, far away. "Yes," Andi would say begrudgingly, giving Nate a withering look with the corners of her eyes. "I suppose."

I completed a full draft of my dissertation just after 5 p.m. on my twenty-eighth birthday. The moment I hit "save" and emailed the document to my committee chair was sheer euphoria—the best birthday present I'd ever given myself. But as the burst of delight mellowed into something more stable, a second emotion showed up to keep the first one company. This new emotion wasn't wearing a name tag. It felt a bit like hunger, like a hollow cavity at the base of my sternum that pulled everything else toward it.

Two days later, my State College friends threw me a surprise birthday party of epic proportions. Carrie the TCK had begun scheming months ahead of time, drafting a guest list by casually asking me to name my closest friends in town, slowly stockpiling bananas in her freezer to bake nine loaves of chocolate chip banana bread. Nine loaves might have been a bit excessive to feed thirty-five mouths, although the yells of "Surprise!" as I walked into the room felt loud enough to belong to a ravenous army.

Everyone who heard about my finished dissertation draft celebrated the news with me. "On to the revisions!" they said. "To the defense! To the job market! To the adventure ahead!" They tried to sound as excited for me as they assumed I must be for myself. And I parroted their enthusiasm, trying to sound as eager for my prospective career as everyone else seemed to believe I was.

The party was a deluge of dear friends, a relational feast as well as a culinary one. But after the feasting, the hollow hungry feeling returned, hollower and hungrier than before.

Newly (if temporarily) liberated from academic responsibilities, I snuck into our church building one evening and wrote a song about saying goodbye to people who feel like home. Sitting at the piano, I sang over a roomful of empty chairs as I composed. The hollowness in my chest grew larger and lodged in my throat, until I couldn't sing another syllable.

$$\circ \ \circ \ \circ$$

Despite Andi's threats, I was offered two tenure-track professorships the following year. As I evaluated the offers according to their professional merits, I also googled local churches near each university, scoured their websites, and tried to imagine how I would be received in their congregations as an openly gay and celibate person.

I had never needed to ask this question in quite the same way before. When I moved to State College and chose a local church community to belong in, I was cozily wedged in the closet and had no intention of ever coming out. By the time most of my State College congregation learned I was gay, they'd already known me as a worship leader for three-and-a-half years. My coming out was certainly complicated—but by then, it was too late to ask whether I should have chosen a different church. The congregation and I were already entangled with each other, for better or worse. (For better, as it turned out, in almost every case.)

This time, though, I had to imagine entering a church as someone who would be gay from the very beginning. Not that I planned to announce my gayness with a trumpet fanfare the moment I marched in the door. Still, deep and honest disclosure about my life could only go so far before I'd have to mention being gay. If the people of this new church were going to become like family to me, they'd have to know me. I didn't want to waste time in a church community where I couldn't really belong, and I had no intention of trying to earn my belonging by wedging myself back into a closet I had long since outgrown.

How, I wondered, should I vet prospective churches? Should I simply send an email to each church's pastors, explain my situation, and see whose response I liked best? I felt instinctively unsettled by the confrontational nature of that approach. Why should sexuality be my first conversation with my future pastor, when my day-to-day existence and my spiritual life were predominantly shaped by other, more significant matters?

But the thought of going into a church unannounced nauseated me even more. The thought of blending in for the first month or two, investing time and hope into a few burgeoning relationships, patiently waiting until the topic of sexuality arose organically. Would I discover when that shoe finally dropped that I was too progressive to belong with them? Too conservative? Too outspoken? Too gay?

Would they try to tell me—with their eyes, if not with their words—that someone like me could only ever be a second-class citizen in the kingdom of heaven?

Many of my LGBTQ friends had experienced deep wounding at the hands of their local church communities. They had been treated with heightened scrutiny and suspicion because of their sexuality, urged to stop talking about their experiences and return to the closet, denied or removed from visible service within the church, told that being gay made them more sinful and more fallen than the holy heterosexuals.

I had only ever given one church the opportunity to wound me this way, and they hadn't. On the contrary, they loved me even more (if such a thing were possible) than they'd loved me before I came out. They declared the gospel to me by their words and actions and smiles and embraces: that all of us are equally invited to follow Jesus and to belong in his family. That the story of redemption God tells in each of our lives is a story worth retelling. That there are no second-class citizens in the kingdom of heaven.

I'd played church roulette exactly once, and I had been resoundingly victorious. But just as winning one round of Russian roulette doesn't make the bullet disappear from future rounds, so winning one round of church roulette doesn't erase the terror of the game.

"Leaving is supposed to hurt," my twelfth-grade Bible teacher told our class as we were preparing to graduate from high school. "If you tear off your finger, it's supposed to hurt. That proves it's been attached to you for all these years."

In the weeks before I graduated and left for college, I made an effort to thank as many of my Indonesia-dwelling friends as I could for the ways their friendship had been meaningful to me. During that process, I realized that the more eager I was to thank someone—the more meaningful our friendship had been—the more painful the thought of departure became. When I thanked people for entangling their lives with mine, for belonging with me and letting me belong with them, I might as well have been saying, "Thank you for making me hurt."

As Winnie-the-Pooh is often (though falsely) purported to have said—and as, therefore, I imagine my father reading aloud in his half-asleep drawl—"How lucky I am to have something that makes saying goodbye so hard."

○ ○ ○

For a year I grieved, as I anticipated the loss of my beloved community in State College. I celebrated the relational gifts I had been given, and I thanked them for making me hurt. I traveled to two lovely job interviews on two lovely campuses and received two lovely offers. Everyone, myself included, assumed that I would say yes to one of them.

And then I didn't say yes to either one.

It would take too long, and get us thoroughly off topic, for me to explain all the factors that went into my decision to step back (at least temporarily) from the academy. All you need to know for our current purposes is that, instead of bidding my church farewell, I accepted a part-time job there. The loss of local community that I was grieving never came. Quite the opposite. Suddenly I was able to dedicate more time than ever to my church, and to spend the remaining balance of my time writing and editing and speaking about topics near and dear to my heart.

If I'd had a dream job as a child—if I'd had a dream life—it might have been something like this one.

Lest I make everything sound too rosy and optimistic, I should also say that this central Pennsylvanian church family of mine still isn't perfect. (As a wise former pastor of mine used to say, "If you find the perfect church, don't join it; you'll ruin it.") I've been given plenty of opportunities to feel slighted, misunderstood, and excluded. There are any number of ways in which, if I had total authority, I'd want to invent a different church than the one I have. But most of the time, when I'm at my wisest, I choose to celebrate the beauty of what I've been given instead of searching for reasons to feel out of place.

"Don't walk through the world looking for evidence that you don't belong," says Brené Brown, "because you will always find it."

As I look toward my now-indefinite future in State College, I have a hunch that this new job situation—my haphazard cocktail of leading worship and authoring and making buttercream icing at a local bakery—won't last forever. Perhaps it will persist for another year or two. Perhaps longer. Perhaps less. But sooner or later, the goodbyes I've narrowly avoided might still need to be spoken.

The beautiful thing about the people who become our home is that they give us strength to grieve their farewell when the time comes. Even as they increase our potential for pain by letting us grow attached, they make us into the kind of people who grieve from a place of confident belonging. They may tear our hearts to shreds at the moment of departure, but they are also the thread in the hands of the One who faithfully stitches us back together again.

○ ○ ○

I don't know exactly how old my friend Jane Crandell is, and it's probably not polite to ask. But she is, by her own report, "pretty old." A halo of snow-white hair curls tightly around her head, and she's been a stalwart leader in my State College church for at least as long as I've been alive.

"Where have you been?" she chides me from her perch behind the welcome desk in the church lobby. "I haven't seen you in ages."

"Last week I was speaking at a conference," I protest. "But I was here two weeks ago. Where were you?"

She chuckles like a mischievous fourth grader caught in the act of a prank. "I guess I wasn't here two weeks ago. I got sick. But I was healthy last Sunday, and I missed you. People asked where you were. You're very popular around here, in case you didn't know."

"I haven't ascended to Jane Crandell levels of popularity," I tell her with a wink.

Without a hint of hubris, she nods in agreement. "That's true. I am popular. When you're as old as me, you can't help knowing a few people."

I tell her that I'm writing a new book about belonging. She gasps, leaning over the welcome desk and grabbing my hands between hers. "That is so important," she says emphatically, and then says it three more times, seeming to feel the words afresh with each iteration. "That is so important. That is so important. That is so important, because a lot of people don't even feel like they belong *here*."

She lingers on the word *here*, waving a hand toward the rest of the church building and the congregation currently gathered in the next room. The thought of people not belonging in our church, in her company and mine, seems to shock her. *If they can't even belong here*, her eyes say—*if they can't even belong among the one group of people who ought to be inviting everyone in without caveats or reservations—what are we doing wrong? And how do we fix it?*

"Belonging with Jesus," she says finally, releasing my hands and sitting back, nodding thoughtfully. "Belonging in the family of God. That's the most important belonging of all. Is that what you're going to tell everyone in your book?"

"Maybe I'll just write about you, Jane," I say, "and let you tell them yourself."

Stitching

My heart is a transplant, and I've grown attached to you
Saying goodbye is like tearing my chest into two
You've been home what feels like forever
I'm not sure where I could ever belong instead

We celebrate birthdays, tell stories for hours unplanned
I know your laugh like the veins on the back of my hand
You've been home, without you I'm homesick
Terrified that I won't find it again

Is home just a dream that I have been dreaming?
Is it a hoax I'm bent on believing?
Or is it the thread stitching my tattered heart together today?

I'd almost forgotten the sorrow that love can exert
The memories I cherish are the same memories making me hurt
You've been home, and home feels so fragile
Gone so swift, arriving so gradual

Is home just a dream that I keep on dreaming?
Is it a hoax I'm bent on believing?
Or is it the thread stitching my tattered heart together?
I try to forget but can't live without it
Know it for years and somehow still doubt
This invisible thread stitching my tattered heart together

If I say thank you for this family
That you are to me
I guess I'm thanking you for making me hurt
Thank you for making me hurt

Because home's where we'll wake when we finish dreaming
A promise of love we're made to believe in
The thread in the hands stitching our tattered world back together
For forty more breaths as I sit here grieving
Forty more hours till my flight is leaving
Forty more years till I punch the clock, if I last that long
As long as it takes, till you and I finally forever belong

PART THREE

Belonging To

If we have no peace, it is because we have
forgotten that we belong to each other.

Teresa of Calcutta

Magnets

I said farewell to my reputation on a Monday evening in February. The Facebook post had been written since December, but I promised Aaron I would give him a chance to talk to the elders of our church before I posted it. For two months, the announcement sat in the Drafts folder of my email account, growing more potent in my imagination as it aged, ripening like a cheese:

Dear friends,

I'm delighted to announce that I have a book coming out with InterVarsity Press this August! But given the book's topic, I should probably mention a few other things too:

(1) I'm gay. (2) Because of my commitment to follow Jesus and the way I understand the Bible, I'm choosing to remain celibate. (3) No matter who you are, I continue to love you just as I always have. If you're LGBTQ and pursuing same-sex sexual expression or marriage, I love you. If you're a Christian who's troubled or offended by my very existence as a gay man, I love you. If you think I've gotten Jesus or my sexuality all wrong, I love you. Perhaps you'll stop loving me, and that will break my heart, but I won't stop loving you.

If you're full of questions for me, perhaps I can interest you in a forthcoming book, now available for preorder on Amazon.

One closing request: if you feel the need to say something less-than-delightful to me about all this, please do it privately. I don't want to stifle you, but I want this space to remain as safe as it possibly can for the people I love all over the messy, glorious spectra of theology and sexuality.

The Amazon link at the end of the announcement displayed my book cover, a gray outline of half my face beside the words *Single, Gay, Christian*. When my editor first showed me the cover to get my approval, I wanted to object: "But it's my face!"

Then again, I concluded after a few hours of angst, it was also my name on the cover. It was my life. Why shouldn't it be my face?

I obsessed over every word I had written in that Facebook post and the corresponding book, imagining the vast and contradictory range of ways people might respond. The conservatives, I worried, would find me far too progressive, and the progressives would find me far too conservative. Every camp seemed prone to vilify people whose thinking was not identical to their own; and I, to the best of my knowledge, thought identically to almost no one.

I fantasized that if I found the perfect words, I could preclude every objection and keep the whole world happy. I could stand in the chasm between crowds, making everyone feel simultaneously loved and respected and understood. But each time I assuaged one set of possible concerns, I seemed to invite a new onslaught of criticism. I softened the blow toward one crowd only to fan the flames of another.

People-pleasing was one of my first and most enduring talents. I mastered the art of selective self-presentation, learning to emphasize whichever of my traits were most palatable to a given crowd while minimizing the bits of me that wouldn't please them. At the age of twenty-six, I was at the height of my game. When people needed a leader, I took charge and pretended to want authority. If the mission brief called for followers, I could be the sheepiest of sheep. My academic colleagues knew me as open-minded, intellectually curious, and unusually smiley for a grad student. Among evangelicals, I was a golden boy: biblically literate, musically competent, excited about Jesus, comfortable on a stage. I knew when to talk about politics, when to talk about theology, when to be lighthearted, when to sit in silence and let someone else do the talking.

I knew how to manage my reputation. I knew a recipe for disaster when I saw one.

That Monday evening in February, alone in my apartment, I sat at my laptop with my finger poised over Facebook's "Post" button. I read and reread the four little paragraphs that spelled the end of my carefully controlled reputation. The moment after I clicked "Post," I slammed down the laptop lid and sat pressed against the back of my chair, as if I was on the climb hill of a roller coaster. I breathed too fast, feeling suddenly hot in the face and cold in the chest, waiting for the moment I would teeter over the roller coaster's peak and the world would blur out of control.

My phone started buzzing. The blur began.

On roller coasters, there's a fine line between exhilaration and terror.

o o o

I've always aspired to be likable. When my twelfth-grade Bible teacher asked our class to make a list of the ten highest ideals in our lives, I gave the number four slot to "Being Nice." I worried, upon completing the list, that "Being Nice" might be a shallow and insufficiently Jesus-y goal. Then again, I reasoned, too many Christians (both historical and contemporary) had used Christianity as an excuse for heinous and selfish behavior. I would be a Christian who balanced the scales by bearing witness to the kindness and gentleness of Jesus. I would be likable, and people would like me so much that they wanted to like Jesus too.

I never dreamed I would turn into the sort of person who receives occasional hate mail. I never dreamed I would find myself called into the middle of a fiery conflict, reluctantly accruing enemies on both sides of the battlefront. But God has a screwy sense of humor.

I don't disagree with my high school self that following Jesus ought to be attractive to people. Love, joy, peace, patience, kindness, goodness, faithfulness, gentleness, self-control—Paul's list of fruits of the Spirit in Galatians 5:22-23 would fit well in a how-to book on likability. Jesus was wildly attractive to huge masses of people. Would it be such a wonder if his followers carried at least a trace of that same allure?

On the other hand, Jesus also made ferocious enemies. He was magnetic in both senses, repelling as well as attracting. His most important work happened not through his accolades but through a death sentence. Would it be such a wonder if Jesus' followers garnered the same vitriol—if we, like bits of metal in the presence of a magnet, became magnets ourselves?

A good reputation is a great thing when it happens as a by-product of our obedience to Jesus. But reputations, when pursued as ends in themselves, are poor companions to obedience. We too easily wind up trying to please everyone, sacrificing sincerity for palatability, misguidedly protecting the gospel from its own radical weirdness. We too easily take the gold trinkets of other people's opinions and melt them into a golden calf, remaking the gift of God into the object of our worship.

"Woe to you," says Jesus in Luke 6, "when everyone speaks well of you." I used to worry, back before the evening of that fateful Facebook post, that perhaps everyone was speaking too well of me. I'm less worried now.

o o o

If you're looking for tips on coming out as gay and celibate, I don't recommend doing it the way I did, by writing a controversial memoir and turning your private life into a public spectacle for strangers to debate on social media. I certainly don't recommend googling yourself afterward, tallying up all the times you've been called a heretic or an apostate, the book reviews and podcasts and radio broadcasts dedicated to proving how little you love Jesus.

"Whatever you do," my wise author friend Heather advised me, "*don't* read about yourself online. Or if you must do it, do it once, get it out of your system, and never do it again. You're already getting enough criticism you *can't* avoid. Why make yourself miserable reading criticism you *can* avoid?"

She was right, and I knew it—so naturally, I ignored her advice. Once I started paying attention to the naysayers, I couldn't seem to stop. People's anger toward me was irresistible the way candy corn is irresistible. (Every time I eat candy corn, I remember after the first mouthful how disgusting it is, like sweet candle wax colored with crayons. And still I keep eating it, hating myself with every bite, a loathing that is also an insatiable desire.)

Besides, my new reputation wasn't all bad. In addition to the people who hated me, there were people who loved me, often far more effusively than I deserved. And there were people who regarded me as an oddity, neither hero nor villain but something morally neutral, like a circus monkey wearing spangled pants.

I gorged myself on people's opinions, reading and rereading, not sure what held my gaze except my own perverse narcissism. I had thought I was done caring about my reputation. I thought I'd said goodbye once and for all. But it turned out I still cared what people thought about me. I cared more than ever.

In the old days, my mission had been to make everyone happy, and I had believed it was possible to succeed. Every time I was criticized, I would alter something about myself in response, hoping I could eventually appeal to everyone. But when my book came out (and I came out with it), I realized for the first time that someone will always dislike us for the very same reason someone else admires us. We don't get to choose whether we're criticized. All we choose is whose criticism we're going to trust.

Googling myself, I learned that Gregory Coles was both "unflinchingly humble" and "disgustingly arrogant." His story was "gut-wrenchingly hard" but also "quite easy." His book was both "thoroughly biblical" and "blasphemous," "too self-centered" but also "not a self-centered book." He was "honest" but "insincere," "gracious" but "condescending," "joyful" but "whiny," "winsome" but "utterly offensive."

Reputations are like surveys, given to the whole crowd regardless of expertise, with every opinion holding equal weight. It's easy, when the poll numbers are in our favor, to root our sense of belonging in our good reputations. But if we only feel at home when everyone likes us, we'll never truly be at rest. A home built on reputation is no sturdier than a foundation laid in Jell-O.

○ ○ ○

Jesus could have learned a thing or two from the Pharisees about maintaining an upstanding reputation. The Pharisees were masters of self-presentation, experts at keeping their religious bona fides well polished. They knew which words sounded holiest, which parties to attend or avoid, which robes had the longest tassels and which sackcloth was best for advertising a fast. If you surveyed the Jewish world in the early first century and asked who was winning at spirituality, the Pharisees would have been favored contenders.

Jesus, on the other hand, had a pesky habit of hanging out with the lowlifes of society, getting tarnished with muck and guilt by association. The survey numbers on Jesus were mixed, and he didn't waste much time defending his reputation. He didn't dress the part of a rightful king, didn't tell everyone again and again how perfect he was. He simply kept living like himself in the midst of opposition. He kept acting like the Son of God.

Before I signed the contract for *Single, Gay, Christian*, my prescient agent, Mike, made me promise to stay "humble and noncombative" in the face of criticism. One practical implication of my promise was that I chose to never publicly rebut any of the book's critics. Saying nothing felt like a slow death, like watching a wound bleed without reaching for a bandage. I hated being unable to set the record straight. (Though perhaps *straight* is the wrong word.) But as I bled, I realized the only thing dying was my own obsession with being thought well of.

There's something remarkably awful and wonderful about being accused of not really loving Jesus, and then responding simply by continuing to love Jesus anyway.

I said farewell to my reputation on a Monday evening in February, and I've been saying farewell ever since. I'm not done caring what people think of me. I have so much pride left to bleed out. But on the other side of this slow death, I hear the whisper of the only voice that matters, welcoming me into the world I was made for, the place I will belong once and for all.

That Guy Who Cleaned My Microwave

Notes from an Alien Anthropologist:
The human creatures claim they want to invest their lives in things that matter. Upon learning what matters, however, they often decide to invest their lives elsewhere instead.

One of the unwritten rules of being a good houseguest is that you should never spontaneously clean your host's microwave. For this reason, among others, I am not an exemplary houseguest.

It's not that I have a serial habit of microwave cleaning. (Anyone who has seen my apartment can attest that obsessive cleanliness is not a burden I bear.) But whenever I'm at a social event where I feel out of place, I start looking around for a role to play: taking people's coats, chopping crudités, pouring drinks, washing dishes. Anything to justify my presence. Anything to silence the self-conscious voice in my head whispering, "What are you even doing here?"

The microwave-cleaning incident happened in 2008. I had just moved back to the United States for college, and—in my defense—I was still learning to interpret American social cues. I was awaiting my first American wedding, hanging out with the groom and his groomsmen in the groom's older sister's living room. I wasn't part of the bridal party; I was just the piano player, sent by default to hang out with the groomsmen by virtue of my maleness. I'd only met the groom a few times, and his family and friends were mostly strangers to me. My introversion was in a state of emergency, sirens blaring, demanding my exit at the first possible opportunity.

To make matters worse, we were watching reality television. I was new to American television, and watching it required a skill I hadn't yet developed. Everyone else in the living room appeared to be enjoying themselves. I was the only one flinching at each abrupt new sound, each sudden scene change, each exaggerated relational crisis. In this cultural bonding ceremony, I was the obvious outsider, like the guy who attends a barn dance in a tuxedo.

When the groom's sister volunteered to make us some pizza bagel bites, I leaped to my feet. "Can I help?" I said, more a plea than an offer.

"It's not hard," she said. "They just need to go in the microwave."

She was probably trying to say no, but I took her words as a yes. "I'm great at microwaving," I said, as if she had been needing this reassurance.

Once I'd been let into the kitchen, one thing led to another. I noticed that the inside of the microwave was less than immaculate. After the bagel bites were hot, I browsed the cupboards for a roll of paper towels, took out the rotating tray, and got to work. Ten minutes later, the groom's sister came in, probably to figure out what I was doing.

"Are you cleaning my microwave?" she said.

"Yeah, do you have a sponge I could use? This is my third paper towel, and there's more work to be done."

Resignedly, she gave me the sponge, and I gave her the cleanest microwave either of us had seen in years.

Years later, her brother the groom told me, although she had long since forgotten my name, she still remembered me as "that guy who cleaned my microwave."

On one level, I'm embarrassed by my eighteen-year-old self. After a decade or so in the United States, I'm more aware of the social implications of my faux pas. It turns out that if you waltz into someone's house and start cleaning their microwave, it can be interpreted as any of several rude nonverbal messages:

1. "Your house is filthy."

2. "Clearly you are incompetent to address this filth, and I must take matters into my own hands."

3. "You are so interminably boring to me that I would rather perform a tedious household chore than spend one moment longer in your presence."

Still, I sympathize with microwave-cleaning Greg. I wasn't *trying* to communicate any of these things. I didn't mean to be odd and unmannerly. I simply felt out of place, and the microwave was my coping mechanism. I was in search of a role I could fit in. I was trying to make my presence matter.

Better to be the guy who cleaned the microwave than to be nothing at all.

○ ○ ○

In Genesis 3, as God is pronouncing the ways human disobedience has altered the world, he declares that human work has been transformed into something unpleasant: "Cursed is the ground because of you; through painful toil you will eat food from it all the days of your life. It will produce thorns and thistles for you, and you will eat the plants of the field. By the sweat of your brow you will eat your food until you return to the ground" (vv. 17-19).

Those of us who live in a post–Genesis 3 world have only ever known human work as it exists under this curse. It can be hard for us to remember that work was introduced to humankind before the devastation of the fall, one chapter earlier, in Genesis 2. After God models his own rhythms of work and rest at the beginning of the chapter, he assigns work to Adam in verse 15: "The Lord God took the man and put him in the Garden of Eden to work it and take care of it." In Adam's perfect, uncursed life, when everything is functioning exactly as it was designed to function, Adam already has a job to do.

The plan for human belonging includes purposes for each one of us to accomplish, vocations to which we are called. Our work may not always come with a paycheck, because sometimes the most important vocations are those least celebrated by the people around us. And our work might be burdensome at times, because painful toil comes with the territory of the post–Genesis 3 world. But whatever our vocations look like, however enjoyable or laborious, each of us is called to collaborate with God's creative work in our world.

Without vocations—without chasing the purposes we were created for—we're doomed to wander aimlessly, wallowing in ennui, never fitting anywhere.

O O O

"Prophecy is the worst of the spiritual gifts," I once told my parents. "High risk, low pay."

I was in high school at the time, and I was familiar enough with the Bible to know that I was *supposed* to be excited by the prospect of prophecy. "Eagerly desire gifts of the Spirit," says the apostle Paul, "especially prophecy" (1 Corinthians 14:1). But when my parents informed me that they thought I might have some prophetic gifting, and perhaps a bit of prophetic calling on my life to go with it, I didn't receive their observation as good news.

"If I'm a prophet," I told my mother, trying to think of the most outlandish scenario I could imagine, "you'll see a red-haired stranger at church today."

Native Indonesians all have black hair, with the exception of the occasional white-blond albino. Even among the infrequent light-skinned foreigners in our city, red hair was an anomaly. It seemed like a safe enough prediction to demonstrate my prophetic ineptitude.

When we reconvened over lunch, my mother was giddy with excitement. "There was a woman at church with hair dyed bright red!" she announced.

I sputtered into my milk. "I meant *naturally* red hair," I objected. "And I was picturing a male stranger, not a female stranger."

"But that's not what you said, is it?" My mother smirked. "You can't add new stipulations now. You said a red-haired stranger, and that's what I saw."

Whether I actually turned out to have any prophetic gifting or calling is irrelevant for our purposes here. All I knew at the time was that prophecy was a gift I wasn't keen on receiving. The prophets of the Bible seemed to have a pretty raw deal: cooking food over cow dung, wandering around nude for three years, giving names to their children that would merit a call to Child Protective Services today. (Who names a baby "Not Loved"?)

Biblical prophets didn't lead glamorous lives. They didn't go around predicting the outcomes of sports games and doing tarot readings and being featured in documentaries about extrasensory perception. Instead, they spoke incisive and unpopular truths as God commanded them, only to be mistreated and reviled and murdered by the very people who should have been listening to them.

I didn't understand how anyone could eagerly desire such a thing, even after being commanded by the apostle Paul to desire it. As far as I was concerned, the gift of prophecy was bad news for its recipients.

High risk. Low pay.

And yet Paul calls prophecy a gift, despite its potential unpleasantness. It's not a gift given primarily for the pleasure of the recipients, to fill us up with the warm fuzzies. It is, instead, a vocational gift, a means by which God intends to make us a gift to the people around us. Prophecy isn't given for the sake of the prophet; it's given for the sake of the world.

Earlier in 1 Corinthians, Paul has the chutzpah to call celibacy a gift as well. And like prophecy, I'm not always keen on the gift of celibacy. It's not the kind of thing I would put on my Christmas wish list. It doesn't always fill me with the warm fuzzies.

But I'm coming to believe that celibacy, like prophecy, isn't meant to be a gift given primarily for the pleasure of the recipients. I'm coming to believe that celibacy is part of the work God has purposed for some of his followers, the means by which he intends to make us a gift to the people around us. Perhaps the gift of celibacy is given not for the sake of the celibates, but for the sake of the world.

Before you married and nonprophetic folks cheer too loudly about having dodged those two bullets, ponder this: What if marriage, too, is a gift in the style of prophecy and celibacy? What if God's primary purpose for your marriage is not the warm fuzzies you enjoy with your spouse, but rather the ways in which you are meant to become a gift to those around you? What if your marriage is a gift given for the world's sake, and not for your own happiness or comfort?

Maybe you and I struggle to find our sense of purpose in the world—our vocation, our belonging—because we're busy looking for the wrong kind of gifts. Maybe we keep chasing the warm fuzzies instead of brazenly inviting God to make us a gift to others, to give us vocations even when they're uncomfortable—when they're high risk, low pay.

I don't always like my vocations. I don't always like celibacy, or writing, or leading worship, or any of the handful of other tasks to which I feel called by God. These things often feel heavy and hard. They feel like work, in the post–Genesis 3 sense of the word. But when I embrace my vocations, I encounter the joy that comes with living on purpose, the joy of belonging to a meaning more meaningful than me.

"But are you sure that you *really* have the gift of celibacy?" people sometimes ask me.

"There are some gifts," I always respond, "that you wish came with gift receipts."

○ ○ ○

My friend Cady once tried to throw a surprise birthday party for her boyfriend, Jon. She flew up from Kentucky to Pennsylvania without telling him, showed up on his doorstep, and then lured him over to a mutual friend's house where thirty of us waited with cupcakes and chips and balloons to wish him a happy birthday.

After we all yelled "Surprise!" and exchanged hugs and mingled for a few minutes, Cady noticed that her guests were acting strangely. We began slowly drifting down to the basement. Some of us stared at her as we disappeared.

Six of Cady's friends approached her, one by one, each handing her a photograph that signified part of Cady and Jon's dating relationship. Then those six friends drifted down to the basement as well, one by one, until Cady and Jon and a sneakily placed photographer were the only people left upstairs.

Down in the basement, the party guests waited with bated breath for the words we knew were coming: "She said yes!"

Cady had thought she was throwing a surprise birthday party for Jon. In reality, Jon was throwing a surprise engagement party for Cady. He had orchestrated the whole thing, pulled the strings from the very beginning. He conspired with Cady's closest friends in Pennsylvania to plant the idea of a surprise birthday party in her mind. He worked with her friends to direct her to the perfect venue, the perfect time, the perfect guest list. Every detail Cady thought she was choosing had already been chosen for her by her future fiancé.

Sometimes I wonder if we do the same thing to God. We think we're orchestrating the details of our lives on his behalf, trying to do the kind of work we assume will please him. "Look at everything I'm achieving for you," we say proudly. And when we find ourselves called to vocations that don't fit our master plan, we dismiss them. "Surely you wouldn't call me to *that*, God," we shudder. "That would ruin all the plans I've perfectly orchestrated on your behalf."

But the only way we'll ever truly hear the call of God in our lives—the only way we'll be ready to receive the vocations we're created for—is if we become willing to hear *any* answer from God. God is in search of followers who follow any order, however dangerous or dull the work might be, however simple or complex, however invisible or ignominious. Perhaps we struggle to hear God's call because we've only given him permission to say things he has no interest in saying.

Even when it looks like we're the ones throwing a party on God's behalf, he's always the mastermind pulling the strings. Our job as human beings has never been to conjure up a purpose for ourselves. Our job is simply to receive the vocations we are given, to find our place in the story God is already telling.

The Art of Neighboring

> **Notes from an Alien Anthropologist:**
> *A shocking proportion of the human creatures, when they encounter one another for the first time, will each choose to pretend that the other does not exist. The more this fantasy is perpetuated, the truer it becomes.*

Here's an excerpt from an actual text message conversation I once had with a wrong number:

HIM: Hey what's going on?

ME: I'm currently pondering the mystery of whose number this is! How about you?

HIM: It's Henry!!

ME: How delightful! I know and love a number of Henrys! Which one are you?

HIM: [Last name redacted for privacy]

ME: I hate to tell you this, Henry [Last name redacted for privacy], but I don't think you're one of the Henrys I know and love. (Not yet, at any rate.)

HIM: Oh well I must have the wrong number.

ME: Indeed. But I hope you have a lovely evening all the same.

HIM: Aww that's very kind of you.

HIM: You must not be Kyle.

ME: I am not even slightly Kyle. My name is Greg. (But I know and love a number of Kyles.)

HIM: You must know and love a number of people.

ME: I certainly aspire to.

HIM: That's a good aspiration. I just wanna wake up in the morning.

According to the rules of normal conversation, we should have stopped texting at that point, if not ten or twelve sentences sooner. But I've never been one to be plagued by the rules of normal conversation. And neither, apparently, has Henry.

Two hours later we were still sending messages back and forth, posing questions, exchanging thoughts and emojis. I began to construct a mental image of the Kansas City–dwelling twentysomething on the other end of the line. At one point I asked him to compare his personality to a vegetable, and he chose a pickle. "I may look like a cucumber," he said, "but I'm full of flavor."

I told him I was more like a rutabaga: "A good taste, to be sure, and slightly unusual, but not nearly as exciting as the first impression might have suggested."

Our conversation carried over into the next day, the day after that. The following week. The following month. Sometimes we talked about quotidian things: our mutual love of autumn, his regular morning jogs before work, my nightly bowls of cereal before bed. Sometimes the conversation turned deeper, to the places we found joy, our recent triumphs and regrets, the relationships and beliefs and ideals that mattered most to us. I told him about my experience of being gay and celibate, and he told me some of his own experience of sexuality. (But that's his story to tell, so if you're curious, you'll have to text him yourself.)

To this day—or at least, as of the time I'm writing this sentence—Henry and I still stay in touch. We might go for long stretches of time without communicating, but sooner or later, one or the other of us will reignite the conversation, texting a greeting out of the blue. "Have you eaten your cereal this evening?" he'll sometimes ask—and if I'm mid-bowl, I'll text him a picture to prove that I'm a creature of near-absolute habit.

It would have been easy, on the evening of those first text messages, for either of us to simply stop writing the other back. As soon as we realized that we were strangers to one another, we could have chosen to stay strangers, the way most people do when there's a wrong number involved. After all, I was not even slightly the Kyle he was looking for, and he wasn't one of the Henrys I knew and loved.

Not yet, at any rate.

○ ○ ○

The first neighbor I met in my grad school apartment complex was named John. It was a cold autumn evening, well after dark, and I was trying to shave ten seconds off my commute by abandoning the sidewalk and cutting between two buildings. What I'd forgotten—and couldn't see in the dark—was that a strip of concrete ran between those two buildings, rising three inches off the grass, like a sidewalk from nowhere to nowhere. I caught the tip of my shoe on it and went flying, knees thudding heavily on the concrete, my book-stuffed backpack sailing up past my head and carrying me face-first into the dirt.

For a moment I was so disoriented I couldn't move. My knees bled beneath the legs of my jeans.

"Oh shit!" someone yelled. Feet pounded toward me, and I felt a hand on my shoulder. "Are you hurt?"

I turned sideways, reaching for my glasses. "My ego, primarily," I said.

The stranger looked to be about my age, brown-haired and wiry. "I was just walking home when I heard the thud and saw you go down," he said as I slowly sat up. "It's not your fault. I don't know why this stupid sidewalk is here. Who puts a sidewalk through a patch of grass for no stupid reason?" He used a different word for *stupid*, raising our conversation's rating to at least PG-13. I was in enough pain that I wasn't about to disagree with his assessment.

We exchanged names as he helped me stagger to my apartment, with my arm draped heavily over his shoulders. "If you need anything," he said, depositing me at my door, "I'm just two doors down."

When I think of the word *neighbor*, John's face is the image that pops into my mind. I think of how I made pumpkin muffins for him and his girlfriend, how he answered the door wearing boxer briefs and then ate a muffin right there in front of me in order to declare it delicious. I think of how, when the igniter on my gas stove stopped working, I went over to borrow a match and John insisted that I take two full matchboxes. Every time we passed each other in the hallway or parking lot, we would call out each other's names, exchanging greetings and stories and well wishes.

For the year that John and his girlfriend lived two doors down from me, I felt like a good neighbor among good neighbors. But John moved out at the end of the academic year, along with Richard from Brazil, who lived upstairs, and Vickie, who was awkward but friendly and loved to vacuum after midnight. The new couple who moved into John's old apartment seemed less interested in being neighbors. They never answered the door when I knocked to offer them cookies. They would scream at each other late at night, she convinced that he was cheating on her with his ex-girlfriend, yelling sordid accusations while he yelled about her insanity. Through two doors and down a carpeted hallway, I heard every vivid detail.

My church went through a sermon series called "The Art of Neighboring," based on Jesus' command to love our neighbors.

Aaron, who was doing most of the preaching, sent us home after the first week with a light green sheet of paper showing a grid of nine houses. "Yours is the house in the middle," he said. "Write the names of the people who live around you. Pray for them this week. Ask God how you can exhibit his love for them."

I left my paper entirely blank—not because I was too lazy to write anything, but because I had nothing to write. I didn't know any of my neighbors' names anymore.

"Sounds like it's time to go meet some people," said Aaron with a laugh, when I mentioned my quandary. I circulated the hallways of my apartment building a week or two later, carrying a box of cupcakes. Only one woman opened her door to me. She seemed suspicious when I explained that I wanted to give her a cupcake just to be kind. She selected one and then closed the door without thanking me, as if she had done me a favor by unburdening me.

What did it mean to love my neighbors, I wondered, if none of the people living in my apartment complex would speak more than three words to me?

In Luke 10, a legal expert presses Jesus to define the word *neighbor.* The man is hoping to justify himself, probably by defining *neighbor* as narrowly as possible so he can pat himself on the back for being nice to the people who live next door. But Jesus frustrates the man's efforts. He doesn't offer a neighborhood map or a zoning ordinance outlining how close two people must live to qualify as neighbors. Instead, he tells a story about two strangers who live far apart—one in Jerusalem, one in Samaria—and yet wind up as neighbors when their paths cross.

The heart behind the command to love our neighbors, Jesus suggests, is that we're simply called to love the people who happen to be in front of us at any given time. If they live two doors down and give us matchboxes and help us limp home on damaged knees, they're neighbors. If they're in the seat beside us on an airplane, sharing our armrest for the next three hours, they're neighbors. Our server at the restaurant we'll never go back to is our neighbor, and so is the homeless veteran holding a cardboard sign on the street corner. The voice on the other end of the customer service call. The series of texts from a wrong number.

Every person whose path crosses ours becomes our neighbor. They become someone we are called to care about in the same manner we care about ourselves. Simply because they are there. Simply because they are human.

It's hard to be friendless when you choose to treat everyone like a friend.

○ ○ ○

In high school, I brought a bag of carrot sticks every day for lunch. I ate other things besides the carrots too—sometimes a ten-thousand-rupiah lunch (roughly one dollar) from the cafeteria, sometimes a peanut-butter-honey-and-raisin sandwich on hefty squares of whole wheat bread. But always carrots.

Most of my lunches were eaten sitting atop my locker on the open-air third floor, where I could feel the breeze and see out past the treetops to the peak of *Tangkuban Perahu*, our local active volcano. I could have eaten in the cafeteria, but the thought of choosing a table to sit at always stressed me out. It was easier to sit by myself, on a completely different part of campus, and let my introvert flag fly proudly.

Whenever someone walked past me at lunchtime—classmates, teachers, janitorial staff—I would greet them with an outstretched Ziploc bag and three words: "Want a carrot?"

Some people took me up on the offer immediately. Others refused or gave me skeptical looks, in which case I'd launch into a kind of sales pitch: "They're great for your dental hygiene, and full of vitamin A to maintain eye health. And I've got lots."

If the first invitation didn't work, the follow-up invitation usually persuaded people to take at least one carrot. (All except my friend

Cassie, who hated carrots with such a vibrant passion that it's a wonder our friendship survived.) And even if the passersby still declined my carrots, the act of offering them gave me an excuse to greet people, to wish them a lovely afternoon, to extend some small kindness in their direction.

By the end of my senior year, I had given away an unconscionable number of carrots and made some surprising friends along the way. The fourth graders took to calling me Mr. Carrot whenever they passed me in hallways. A group of seventh-grade girls started inviting me to sit with them at lunch; I called them by food-inspired nicknames like "Mango," "Pineapple," and "Toast Crumbs." The Indonesian security guards would greet me with mock salutes and ask, "*Masih ada wortol?* Do you still have carrots?"

When I started doling out carrots, it never occurred to me that I was earning people's favor by being nice to them. I wasn't a clever politician enacting a strategy to make friends and influence people. I simply wanted to offer the only thing I had to give, to bring a bit of kindness into people's lives, regardless of whether they were friends or strangers to me. If I had been *trying* to make people like me—if I had been treating kindness like a transaction, a vending machine with reliable inputs and outputs—the plan probably would have backfired.

But my high school carrots taught me that when you choose to be kind to people without expecting anything in return, some of those people will decide to be kind back to you. If you spend your life lavishing love on everyone available, without expecting reciprocation, you might realize in the end that you're more loved by more people than your heart can possibly contain.

Jesus was the definition of a guy who spent his life loving others simply because they were in front of him. He didn't choose some crowds to belong to and others to ignore. He cared as much about the Samaritans and Romans and Syrophoenicians as he did about the Jews who lived on his block in Nazareth. He healed everyone who asked, accepted dinner invitations from all kinds of people.

For Jesus, there were no strangers. Only neighbors. Only people worth loving.

This kind of region-transcending love is what got Jesus killed in the end. But it's also what drew people to him, what made him belong among hundreds of thousands while he wandered the earth like an alien.

You and I may not have quite the same impact on the strangers we meet as Jesus did. But we're invited to follow his example in treating every stranger like a neighbor. We're invited to belong to everyone who crosses paths with us, to give ourselves away without expecting anything in return, one carrot stick at a time.

As we do, perhaps we'll see our alien world transform, bit by bit, into a neighborhood.

Table for One

Notes from an Alien Anthropologist:
The human creatures who believe in an Architect are often the most prone to hating their bodies and what those bodies can do. They seem to have forgotten that the Architect's first act after inventing human bodies was to call them good.

The first time I remember being aware of my body, I was ashamed of it.

I might have been seven or eight years old at the time. The photograph in my hands showed half a dozen boys, all of us frolicking in the shallow end of a swimming pool, all of us shirtless.

All skinny-chested and passably athletic, except one.

You wouldn't have called me fat, unless you used the term loosely. *Pudgy* might have been more accurate, and even that depended on your standard of comparison. But I was clearly wrestling in a different weight class than the rest of the boys in the photo. (Not that I was doing any wrestling, nonathlete that I was.)

None of my siblings before me had been enrolled in the Society for Prepubescent Pudginess. But I had moved to Indonesia as an adorable three-year-old, and my Indonesian neighbors had taken great delight during those early years in lavishing me with gifts of black licorice and cheap chocolate. I would sit with our landlord and his chess-playing buddies on the porch of the nearest *warung* convenience store, entertaining them with my childish antics and near-fluent Indonesian as they entertained me with treats wrapped in crinkly gold film. Between the extra supply of sugar and my preference for reading books over playing sports, it only made sense that I'd gather a bit more stomach insulation than my siblings.

I don't remember anyone telling me to be ashamed of my body. Maybe they did and I just forgot about it, like the eternal optimist I am. Maybe the messages were so subtle that I never stopped to notice them. Or maybe I made them up all by myself—maybe I noticed my difference from the others and decided that being different was a good enough reason to dislike myself.

When I told my mom a few years later, as we walked through the narrow alleys of our Indonesian neighborhood, that I wasn't happy with the way my body looked, she told me not to worry about it. "Being healthy is more important than looking a certain way," she said. "If you decide you want to make different choices about eating and exercising, that's up to you. But also, puberty's probably going to stretch you out, like a piece of gum."

My mother turned out to be right in this prediction, as she was about most things. Over the course of my teenage years, I sprouted above six feet, leaving the majority of my baby fat behind and taking on a shape most people called *skinny*. But bits of fat still lingered, softening my hips, deepening the cavern of my bellybutton. And the rest of the old pudge reappeared like a phantom limb, no longer visible to any eyes except my own, reminding me—just in case I'd forgotten—that the only feeling I knew how to feel about my body was the gentle but persistent whisper of embarrassment.

Puberty brought other things, too—other reasons to feel ashamed of my body. The clear and steady boy soprano voice I'd enjoyed in my youth turned into the staggering peaks and valleys of an electrocardiogram, its pitch always ready to betray me. And far, far worse—especially for a gay kid still wishing to be straight— the unwelcome signs of sexual arousal, involuntarily making their appearance in my teenage cargo pants at the worst possible times. No matter how fervently I prayed against them, no matter how fiercely I tried to unwrite the wiring of my brain, my pubescent body refused to be told what to do.

Sexuality had taken up residence in me, and I was ashamed of that too.

I started covering up as many body parts as I could, swimming with a shirt on, preferring pants to shorts and long sleeves to short sleeves, even in the Indonesian heat. I tried to forget that anything existed underneath the fabric. I didn't want to be made up of skin flecked with pimples, didn't want to be the owner of a chest or an abdomen, of thighs or genitals. I wanted to be a disembodied brain and a pair of eyes framed by glasses. Just that. Nothing more.

I only knew how to feel one thing about my body.

o o o

Celibacy, when I first considered pursuing it, seemed like the obvious way to handle a body I'd only ever been ashamed of. How better to cope with the naked skin I disdained than to permanently hide it away from everyone?

This, I later realized, is a terrible rationale for celibacy. Or at least, it's a terrible rationale for *healthy* celibacy. Maybe it works okay for people who don't mind stewing in a miasma of their own self-hatred, people content to shut themselves off from God and others in resentful isolation. But celibacy rooted in bodily shame won't work for me, because it contradicts the fundamental truth that makes Christian celibacy worth living: that God takes extravagant, passionate delight in the embodied human creatures he sculpted out of dust.

If celibacy can possibly be good, it can only be good because those of us who pursue it have fallen into a torrid love affair with our Creator. We who are celibate for Jesus are called to be celibate with our whole bodies—not arbitrarily or haphazardly, but purposefully—because Jesus is an eager bridegroom who wants us all to himself. We are called to surrender ourselves up to a Lover who has been whispering into our ears about the beautiful goodness of our bodies since the moment in Genesis 1 when he first laid eyes on us.

The God of the universe has declared over you and me—the embodied you and me, the you and me beneath our clothes, the you and me on the other side of the mirror—that we are created very good. It would be astoundingly arrogant of us to hear that opinion from God and then to continue treating our bodies as a wellspring of shame.

We love—not only others, but also ourselves—because he first loved us.

Because God is not ashamed of his creation, we no longer need to be ashamed of ourselves. Because we belong to God, we are free to belong to ourselves as well, to enjoy our own company, to honor our bodies as temples of the Holy Spirit. We don't need to fear being alone with ourselves, because we no longer feel like our own worst enemies.

When we escape the vicious cycle of self-loathing, we're better equipped to lavish kindness and affection on others. "Loving our neighbors as ourselves" isn't much of an accomplishment if we love ourselves so little that we barely love our neighbors either. To get in the habit of loving every human being created in God's image, we've got to love the human being we know best. Loving ourselves is by no means the whole substance of Christian love, but it is necessarily part of the journey.

We'll never truly belong anywhere, with anyone, or to anything, until we first learn to belong to the lives and bodies and vocations we've been given.

○ ○ ○

"How do you feel about the Song of Solomon?" my friend Bethanne asked me one evening. "Does it feel irrelevant to you as a celibate person? Why do you think it's in the Bible?"

I was at their house doing laundry, as usual. Ben was out of town for a conference, and the kids were in bed, but Ben's mom, Robin, was with us, visiting from Texas yet again to help with the kids.

"Well," I said cautiously, "the Song of Solomon certainly gives us an image of how romantic and erotic love between husband and wife is supposed to look. But I think that image is meant to point us toward something even more significant. The New Testament authors compare the relationship between Jesus and his followers to a marriage relationship. And that's a risky comparison to make, given how many different cultures the Bible is read in and how many different paradigms those cultures might have for what marriage is supposed to look like. Maybe the Song of Solomon's most significant value is in the way it helps us better understand the metaphor of marriage between Jesus and the church, no matter what our culture says about marriage. We are called to live like the bride of Christ, not just in any old way, but specifically in a Song-of-Solomon-ish way."

"So you think the Song of Solomon is all about Jesus?" said Bethanne, gently prodding me forward.

"I think that's the first priority," I said. "Though of course, it also speaks directly to human spouses, to let them know that their love for each other is meant to be full of steamy erotic desire."

"There sure are some *steamy* metaphors in there," interjected Robin, with the kind of fervor that made it impossible to forget she was a pastor's wife.

Between chuckles, I charged boldly ahead. "But the more seriously we take Jesus as our betrothed groom in the ultimate divine marriage, the more the Song of Solomon has to say to the celibates among us. The steamy desire we see in the Song of Solomon—that desperate all-consuming bodily wanting—teaches us something about the urgent passion we're supposed to feel in our love for Jesus. It teaches us about the urgent passion Jesus feels in his love for us."

My speech had slowed to a testudinate pace, anticipating all the ways my words might be misunderstood. Bethanne and Robin, charitable listeners that they were, seemed unphased. I pressed on. "Certainly, I'm not saying that our relationship with Jesus is meant to be sexual. But I also don't want to make the mistake of skipping over the metaphor too quickly. Our betrothal to Jesus isn't *less* than sexual—it's *more* than sexual, a promise of love so deep and all-consuming that sex is merely a pale human precursor. Those of us who are celibate have the privilege of announcing this betrothal with our bodies right now. We get to anticipate the consummation of heaven with a holy longing on earth."

○ ○ ○

It was my celibate gay friend John Wilson who alerted me to the love poetry of yet another celibate John, the sixteenth-century Spanish friar Juan de la Cruz (John of the Cross). Here's that latter celibate John, in his poem "En una noche oscura" (translated by Marjorie Flower), describing his romance with Jesus in unapologetically Song-of-Solomon-ish terms:

> Dark of the night, my guide,
> fairer by far than dawn when stars grow dim!
> Night that has unified
> the Lover and the Bride,
> transforming the Beloved into him.

> There on my flowered breast
> that none but he might ever own or keep,
> he stayed, sinking to rest,
> and softly I caressed
> my Love while cedars gently fanned his sleep.

Breeze from the turret blew
ruffling his hair. Then with his tranquil hand
wounding my neck, I knew
nothing: my senses flew
at touch of peace too deep to understand.

Forgetting all, my quest
ended, I stayed lost to myself at last.
All ceased: my face was pressed
upon my Love, at rest,
with all my cares among the lilies cast.

For de la Cruz, and for countless other Christian celibates through the centuries, the Song of Solomon instructs its readers in celibacy as well as in marriage. (The Franciscan nun Clare of Assisi, according to her biography *Legenda Sanctae Clarae Virginis*, decided to forsake marriage and join the Franciscan order because her mentor Francis "whispered in her ears of a sweet espousal with Christ, persuading her to preserve the pearl of her virginal purity for that blessed Spouse.")

Celibacy is not an erasure of our capacity to desire whole-bodied intimate devotion. It isn't a resignation to bodily shame, to a life spent wishing that our chests and abdomens and thighs and genitals had never been created in the first place. Though followers of Jesus are called to hate our sexual sin, we are not called to hate the goodness that our sin distorts. Celibacy beckons us not into self-hatred but into the most radical kind of delight, a delight that takes its cue from God's radical delight in us.

Nor is this invitation to find visceral delight in Jesus restricted to single people. Religion scholar Rabia Gregory, in her book *Marrying Jesus in Medieval and Early Modern Northern Europe*, explains that it was common not only for monks and nuns but for all Christians in the Middle Ages to think of themselves as married to Jesus:

When they stood before the altar and gazed at the Crucifix, they saw their spouse; when they swallowed the Eucharistic wafer they embraced their lover; when a medieval Christian heard Christ called "Bridegroom," they recalled the *Song of Songs'* reassurance that "I am my beloved's and he is mine."

Adopting Solomon's love poetry as a model for our romance with God does not mean that we falsely conflate God's love with sexual behavior between human spouses. And yet celibacy is also not a consolation prize for those of us who don't get the better pleasure of physiological sexual consummation. Quite the reverse. To know God as bridegroom—to *know* him in a Song-of-Solomon-ish way—is to participate in a delight so scintillating that no earthly metaphor, not even the thrill of holy erotic love, can begin to do it justice.

Joyful celibacy is rooted in the conviction that our bodies exist to desire and be desired by the paragon of all lovers. To embrace celibacy this way isn't about repressing or sublimating our embodied longing, but about reordering that longing toward its first and best purpose.

○ ○ ○

I spent my first night in California alone. The rest of the weekend schedule was packed full of lunch dates and coffee dates and dinner dates, in addition to the community forum and two church services for which my hosts had flown me across the continent. But that first evening, I had no one sharing Los Angeles with me. I drove myself from airport to hotel in a rental car, then set out on foot toward the local restaurant with the best Google reviews and the fewest dollar signs beside its name.

As I walked the half mile to dinner on deserted sidewalks, drivers of passing cars looked sideways at me. (Los Angeles, as it turns out, isn't the sort of city where people walk places.) It occurred to me that the strange looks I was getting would probably continue when I reached the restaurant. I'd be sitting alone, looking friendless and pitiable, like some poor schlub getting stood up on a date.

I suppose I could have chosen to see myself that way too. As someone waiting for a romance that would never arrive. A case study in loneliness.

But whatever anyone else might have assumed, I chose to believe something different about myself. I was in the company of the Lover of my soul, enjoying a romantic evening alone with him.

"I'm on a date with Jesus," I declared aloud into the crisp evening air. *Now that crazy walking guy is talking to himself too*, the passing drivers must have thought.

"How many?" asked the maitre d' as I stepped inside and pulled off my hat.

"One," I said.

"Table for one?" He held up his index finger incredulously, as if to make sure I had counted properly.

"Table for one," I repeated without flinching. It didn't seem necessary to explain to him that, even though I would only need one menu, I had no intention of dining in solitude.

I can't remember a dinner I've enjoyed more than my first meal in California. Jesus and I had so much to talk about. My fascination with Los Angeles so far. The tastiness of my Santa Fe salad (recommended to me by my waiter). The laughter and chatter of nearby diners. My hopes and plans and fears for the next few days, the next few months, and the next few years.

Twice my waiter stopped by my table, thinking I had been trying to get his attention as he walked past. "You looked like you were communicating with someone," he said. "I thought it was me."

"Thanks for checking," I said. "But no, it wasn't you."

I couldn't stop looking into the eyes staring into mine from across the table. My Lover was so kind, so brilliant, so beautiful. So much better than any boyfriend I could have dreamed up (let alone acquired) for myself.

Under other circumstances, I wouldn't have splurged on dessert, but my waiter offered me a skillet cookie sundae on the house. "For real?" I asked gratefully. "What's the occasion?"

"It's your first time here," he said. "And you look like you're having a really nice night."

"Yes," I said, as he retreated out of earshot. "We are."

Deliciously full, Jesus and I walked home in the darkness, laughing together at the strange glances we collected from passing cars. Back in the hotel room, after a few hours of reading, we climbed into an unfamiliar bed like honeymooners. In the steamiest and most Song-of-Solomon-ish way, his gentle touch wounded me, the jolt from his fingers racing through me like electricity.

19

Limbs

Notes from an Alien Anthropologist:
The human creatures benefit most from the company of companions unlike themselves. When tasked with seeking out their own companions, however, they scour the planet searching for an identical twin.

If Christian denominations were dog breeds, I would be the quintessential mutt. My theological convictions are a collage of Wesleyan and Anabaptist and charismatic and Pietist and Quaker and Anglican and mystic, pasted together like a bad photoshop job. I don't have anything against the theological purebreds; I affirm so much about each breed from which I am descended. But there's no way I could pass for a true denominational stud dog. Every denomination, sooner or later, leaves me saying, "Hang on a moment . . . what about this other bit of truth?"

My hybridity makes it difficult for me to sign doctrinal statements. When I became a member of my current church, I penciled asterisks after two of the ten doctrinal points I was asked to affirm. "I'm not totally opposed to either of these doctrines," I wrote in the margin at the bottom of the page. "But I'm also not 100 percent convinced of either one, and I don't want to pretend to agree with a doctrine that I'm not persuaded is the best reading of the biblical texts."

The elders still let me become a church member, asterisks and all. "We probably won't ask you to preach on eschatology any time soon," said Aaron over breakfast at my membership interview.

Dribbling syrup onto a dry patch of pancake, I laughed. "That's fine. You're a good enough preacher that I'm not about to stage a coup."

I might have been tempted, if such a thing were possible, to erase those asterisks from my brain and heart, so I could be a perfect theological fit within a church I was quickly growing to love. But I've never been good at believing things just because people around me want me to believe them. I've never been able to hibernate my brain long enough to drink anyone else's Kool-Aid.

Don't hear me saying that I think the basic tenets of historic Christianity are up for grabs. Following Jesus isn't a do-it-yourself art project; we can't simply paint with the theological colors we prefer and leaving the rest hidden in their bottles. But the issues that divide Christian denominations from one another—the issues I insist on asterisking in doctrinal statements—are not the basic tenets of historic Christianity. As notable as glossolalia or the pre-tribulation rapture might be in some formulations of Christian doctrine, they have neither the longevity nor the universality of the Apostles' Creed.

I still care deeply about the finer points of theology. What's more, I want to learn from the wisdom of my Christian siblings as I sort out my own theological convictions on these disputed questions. But good theology can't be achieved by way of a strict, draconian system that punishes people for crimethink. My mind and heart will never be committed to a theology that's forced onto me like an arranged marriage.

If I'm going to trust that the truth is true, I need to go out adventuring and stumble across it, to gasp at the beauty of orthodoxy as if I'm discovering it for the first time.

I come by my maverick tendencies honestly. When my dad was in seminary, he told one of his professors that he agreed with lots of denominations about the things they had in common with each other, but he disagreed with them all about the theologies that made them distinctive as denominations.

His professor responded: "Thus speaks the founder of a new denomination."

O O O

My friend Curry isn't the sort of person you'd expect to be named "Curry." He's a white guy from small-town Texas who had never tasted curry until I offered to cook it for him when he was twenty-three years old. ("Shall we eat your namesake for dinner?" I asked, to which he responded, "I beg your pardon?")

Curry was assigned to me by the English Department at Penn State. I was a third-year graduate student, he an incoming first-year graduate student in need of a mentor. I met him and his fiancée, Liz, as I helped them unload their moving truck into the apartment they would begin sharing after their wedding a few weeks later. We enjoyed each other's company so much that, when the truck was empty, I didn't want to leave. I volunteered instead to wash all the unpacked dishes as Liz devised homes for them in her new kitchen cabinets.

I call Curry my Favorite Reformed Friend. He's the sort of person who has read John Calvin's *Institutes of the Christian Religion* cover to cover, keeps a copy on his bookshelf, and can quote it at length from memory. I've got plenty of other Reformed friends, but I don't discuss the distinctives of Reformed theology with any of them nearly as much as I do with Curry.

Once, on our way home from a rhetoric conference in Portland, we spent an entire four-hour flight debating the nature of God's foreknowledge and human will, throwing around words like *soteriological* and *Pelagian*. When we landed in Chicago, the woman sitting across the aisle from us leaned over and said, "Thanks for an enlightening ride."

Like the rhetorical scholars of yore, Curry is an excellent preacher. Despite our theological differences—or perhaps because of them—Curry loves to hear my opinions on the topics of his upcoming sermons. "What would you say," he'll ask, "if you were giving a talk about Jesus as the word made flesh in John 1?" Or, "What would you tell a bunch of college students about why God created sex?" Or, "What passages would you reference if you were preaching to a Southern Baptist church about the necessity of forgiveness?"

I'll sit in silence for twenty or thirty seconds after one of these inquiries, then start saying whatever pops into my head until I come up with something Curry either loves or hates. "I need to write that down," he'll say. Or perhaps, on the other end of the spectrum, "Those are some words I definitely won't say in my sermon."

The night Curry asked for my opinion on the Bible, we had just finished a dinner of Venezuelan black beans. Liz retreated to their bedroom as soon as Curry and I started talking theology, even though we tried to keep her in the living room by proposing other conversation topics. "No, it's okay," she insisted. "I have some work I really need to finish, and if you promise to talk about theology for an hour or so, I won't be tempted to come back and socialize until I'm done."

We promised, and Liz disappeared. That was when Curry asked what I thought about the Bible.

"I'm in favor," I said.

Curry rolled his eyes. "Please elaborate."

I had just finished reading N. T. Wright's fabulous book *Scripture and the Authority of God*, so I offered a sloppy CliffsNotes version. "If we treat the Bible primarily as a collection of correct facts to be believed or disbelieved," I said, "we're not handling it the way it asks to be handled. The Bible is God's authoritative invitation for us to participate in his ongoing narrative of redemption. We're supposed to join the Bible's story, not spectate from a distance."

Curry nodded as he sipped his postprandial tea. "But isn't it still important that we believe the Bible's facts about God correctly, so we can join the story properly? Doesn't the Bible have to put restrictions and limitations on us in order to do its job?"

"Sure," I agreed. "But I think a lot of Christians treat the Bible like it's a leash tied to a stake in the ground, making sure we never go anywhere. I'd argue that the Bible ought to function more like a leash held in the hand of a God who's taking us on a walk. It directs and limits us, not to keep us docile and motionless, but to guide us safely to the places we're called to go. Trusting the Bible should make us bolder and more adventurous, not keep us confined to a seven-foot radius in the back yard."

"Good metaphor," said Curry. By the look on his face, I couldn't tell if he was going to write it down, or if those were some words he definitely wouldn't say in his sermon.

A few days later, after skimming Wright's book again, I sent Curry a text message outlining the kind of sermon I would have wanted to preach if I were in his shoes: "One of the primary reasons we need the Bible is the ongoing discomfort and tension it creates for us, no matter when or where we believe or what doctrinal positions we ascribe to. To the degree that we manage to read the Bible as a reaffirmation of everything we already think and believe, it doesn't have much impact on us. But to the degree that it continually startles and corrects us and places us in tension with itself, it serves as a bastion against the alluring pressures of cultural trend and religious groupthink and our own fleshly impulses."

"Now you're sounding Reformed!" Curry texted back gleefully.

Just to prove he and John Calvin hadn't won me over yet, I replied with a quote from the fabulously un-Reformed N. T. Wright: "To affirm 'the authority of scripture' is precisely *not* to say, 'We know what scripture means and don't need to raise any more questions.' It is always a way of saying that the church in each generation must make fresh and rejuvenated efforts to understand scripture more fully and live by it more thoroughly, even if that means cutting across cherished traditions" (*Scripture and the Authority of God*, p. 92).

Loving the Bible means letting it take us on a journey, daring to discover something new, following its tugging leash even when that leash pulls us past the boundaries of our picket fences and out of our denominational comfort zones into the wide, wild world of the global and historic church.

O O O

I don't think God is surprised by the existence of denominations. I don't think he's up in heaven wringing his hands, bemoaning the varied expressions of Christian faith among people reading the same Bible and seeking to follow the same Savior, outraged that so many of us have gotten him wrong and only one tiny church somewhere in Bolivia has gotten everything entirely right.

I think God knew we'd be different from one another. I think he expected that, among those seeking to follow him, there would be people better or worse equipped to see certain sides of the whole truth, people more or less willing to follow him in certain kinds of obedience, people more or less disposed to fall into certain kinds of errors.

The genius of Christian unity, of the body of Christ acting like a body composed of different parts, is that we become wiser and more whole in fellowship with each other. Our tensions, like tendons, make us able to reach in multiple directions without tearing apart. But if we keep ourselves sequestered in camps of identical theology and culture and practice, we risk devolving from a whole body into a pile of limbs.

Piles of limbs, according to most scientific studies, accomplish very little.

I'm not suggesting that we all need to ditch our denominations and sink into a murky theological swamp together. I'm not saying we should act as if everyone is equally right, as if the truth doesn't matter that much, as if picking a faith tradition were only as significant as picking a favorite holiday beverage or sports team. Rather, I'm proposing that some of the tensions that have torn us into denominations might be design features in the diverse body of Christ rather than flaws.

Some individuals and denominations tend toward emotion, others toward intellection. Some emphasize the redemption of unjust social systems, others the redemption of individual souls. Some prefer to dwell on what can be confidently known by our theology, others on the inevitable mystery we confront as finite minds grappling with infinite realities.

God is big enough to contain the totality of all these spectra within himself. He's bigger than your denomination and mine. His Holy Spirit inhabits not just each individual limb, but also the tensions and tendons that hold us together as a body, as a capital-*C* Church spanning arguments and continents and millennia.

If we're perturbed by the thought that the Spirit could work in *those* people—the people we'd like to forget about, the people whose theology we can't stand—maybe it's because we've tried to tame the Spirit into a calculus equation. But the Spirit doesn't play by the rules of calculus (thank goodness) and has no patience for our taming. As Jesus tells Nicodemus in John 3, the Spirit (*pneuma* in Greek) acts like wind (also *pneuma* in Greek). Both kinds of *pneuma* are unpredictable and uncontrollable. Sometimes choosing to be still in places we were convinced ought to catch the breeze. Sometimes blowing with hurricane force in places we were sure wind could never reach.

If we only ever look for God's fingerprints in the places we expect to find them, we condemn ourselves to ignore some of his finest handiwork.

○ ○ ○

I've been arguing with Rachel Gilson since the moment we met. In her role as a theological Pooh-Bah for a national Christian organization, she had received a copy of my book *Single, Gay, Christian* a few weeks before it was available to the general populace. When she reached out to me by email for the first time, she offered some kind words of camaraderie and shared her own testimony with me. She also began immediately prodding at our differences, pointing to areas of my book she wished had been different, arguing that some of my musings had lacked wisdom and perspective.

I was mostly avoiding fights with strangers in that season of my life. But something about Rachel drew me in. Her reflections— even the ones I didn't like or agree with—were so sincere, so full of humble depth, so clearly motivated by her love for Jesus. I couldn't resist writing her back.

Half of me felt sincerely delighted at the opportunity to correspond with her. The other half of me felt peevish and argumentative. The only thing all of me could agree on was that Rachel was my sister in Christ—that even when she and I stretched in different directions, straining the tendons that held us together, we still belonged to the same body.

She wrote again. I wrote again.

In the following months, the testimony Rachel had emailed to me appeared in a popular Christian magazine, where it garnered a deservedly wide audience. "On second reading," I wrote to her, "this is still delightful. I pray that you're receiving, and continue to receive, much of the joy and encouragement and ministry opportunity that can come from telling a story like this one. (Also, I pray you're not receiving too much of the crap that sometimes accompanies it.)"

She wrote back that she had recently seen me featured in a short film: "It reaffirmed my desire to get to hang out with you someday, because you seem, shall I say, delightful? I'm thankful for your bravery in being out there, and the way God has made you so damn winsome. May it all be for his glory."

Meanwhile, Rachel's kind words and criticisms about my book became an online book review that likewise (to my chagrin) garnered a wide audience. Conservatives seemed to take great delight in ignoring the nice parts of her analysis and augmenting the critical parts, citing her words as proof that I was a dangerous liberal not worth listening to.

In the eyes of the internet, we became one another's anti-matter. I was the anti-Rachel, she the anti-Greg.

"Don't you think," Rachel wrote to me, "if we were just sitting around, people would see that you and I in so many ways line up? We are on the same team. I see you and I as together in the task of ministering, brother. I see this more as you and I having a conversation while we sit in the same dugout as opposed to yelling at each other across the field in different uniforms."

"Perhaps," I wrote in reply, "a few corners of the internet will always be convinced that you and I are fundamentally at odds. As for me, I'm glad to share the dugout with you."

I was still peeved by her book review, still frustrated by our differences, still persuaded that I was more right than she. But more than I wanted to be peeved, more than I wanted to be frustrated, more than I wanted to be right—I wanted most of all to share the dugout with her.

Our differences didn't evaporate as time went on. We continued to think in tension with each other in the dozens of emails that followed. When we spent five hours talking over coffee and sandwiches on a March day as I traveled through Boston, neither of us was under the illusion that the other had thrown up a white flag. When we began plotting future hangouts and texting each other little snarky messages just for fun, we didn't do it because we saw ourselves as finally identical.

Instead, as my affection for Rachel grew, I grew to appreciate more and more the ways in which our tensions with each other were valuable. Rachel cautioned me against dangers that she perceived more clearly than I, pulling me in directions I sometimes needed to be pulled. And I, for my part, cautioned her against dangers foreign to her own experience, nudging her in ways she sometimes needed to be nudged (or so I'd like to believe).

Our tugging was like the tugging of a rope: a tension that, rightly deployed, helps people scale cliffs or saves them from plummeting to their deaths. The rope tugging between us didn't have to tie us down or hold us back. It could hold us together instead, make us a single body stronger than our disjointed limbs could ever be.

Two years after my friendship with Rachel began, I stepped into a pastor's office in San Jose, California, to find Rachel's review of my book open on his computer screen. "Can I take a picture?" I asked eagerly. "I want to text it to Rachel. She'll think it's hilarious."

"You guys are friends?" he said, looking mildly surprised.

"Very much so," I gushed. "She's one of my favorite people in the world."

He looked down at the computer screen, back up at me. "I take it this review didn't end your friendship?"

"Weirdly," I said, "it kind of started our friendship."

○ ○ ○

"If only Christians would stop treating minor theological differences as things meant to divide us," I once told my father. "If only we had eyes to see God at work across denominational lines, to think of ourselves as purposefully different actors in the bigger story God is telling. If only we could all tell our own parts of the gospel story with conviction, without denigrating the people whose convictions lead them to tell a different part of the story. Doesn't that seem better than our current arrangement, all of us sniping at our siblings in Christ and trying to shield our backs from friendly fire? Doesn't that seem like the kind of unity Jesus prayed for in John 17?"

Dad didn't miss a beat: "Thus speaks the founder of a new denomination."

20

Memento Mori

Notes from an Alien Anthropologist:
Life on Planet Earth is best understood in reverse. The human creatures who know the most about living are those who first understand the significance of dying.

I was playing Speed Scrabble the afternoon I found out I was supposed to be dead. We were mid-round when the text message came, which is why no one saw it until a few minutes later. Most of us were still triumphantly or begrudgingly tallying our scores when someone said, "Have you seen this text?"

Two words: "Please pray." Sent at 3:19 p.m.

That was the moment I should have died.

It was July of 2006, the summer before my junior year of high school. Technically, "summer" had no seasonal meaning in Indonesia, only an academic one. Our tropical weather toggled between two seasons: rainy and dry. The rainy season brought six months of hot, humid, sunny days interrupted by an hour or two of torrential rain each afternoon. The dry season brought six more months of hot, humid, sunny days, this time without the interrupting rain.

Still, temperature change or no, a lot of us who grew up with American or European parents (or who read American and European books in school) continued to vaguely associate our passing months with the northern hemisphere's four seasons. In autumn, we ate canned cranberries and made pumpkin-ish pie using the baked flesh of the Indonesian *labu madu* (literally, "honey gourd"). In winter, we cut snowflakes out of construction paper and sang carols over unnecessarily warm mugs of wassail and cocoa. In springtime, we wore bright pastels to church (or the fashionable people did, at any rate) and intoned about April showers bringing May flowers.

In summer, then, I always imagined that the world had a distinctively summery feeling. Though my dad's outdoor thermometer remained unchanged, my psychosomatic thermostat made the summer months seem hotter than all the rest. These were the obvious months for beach trips and gratuitous swimming and watermelon consumption. When I started sweating in the summer months (as I did all year round), I would think to myself, "This just proves it's summertime."

My best friend Zack was visiting from the United States for a few weeks that July. As the pinnacle of his visit, the pièce de résistance, we planned a trip with his dad to the coastal town of Pangandaran. It would be the quintessential summer getaway: Days spent on the beach, racing across scalding sand and throwing ourselves into the merciful coolness of the waves, boogie-boarding and bodysurfing for hours while time stood still. Nights eating fresh-caught shrimp and pungent durian on the side of the street, walking barefoot along still-warm-but-no-longer-scalding sand as gentle tides lapped our feet, playing cards on a breezy hotel balcony fifty meters from the shoreline.

Zack's fever started a few days before our trip was scheduled to begin. First he was unreasonably tired, no longer as hungry as he should have been for all the nostalgic Indonesian meals we were eating together. A few long naps and handfuls of ibuprofen later, we had to admit that he was Officially Sick, complete with pain and chills and vomiting. It was probably dengue fever, or maybe chikungunya, though not such a severe case he needed to be diagnosed or hospitalized. Either way, the treatment was the same: lots of fluids, lots of rest. And absolutely no adventuring to Pangandaran.

With his return flight to the United States looming, there was no time to reschedule the trip for after he recovered. So much for shrimp and boogie-boarding. So much for our pièce de résistance.

Zack spent most of his precious remaining days in Indonesia confined to his bed in the guest room, sleeping whenever he could, lying in agonized silence when he couldn't. I grieved the unfairness of it all in archetypal teenage boy fashion, by suppressing my feelings and playing a lot of computer games.

The day of the text message was a day we should have been at the beach. I wasn't supposed to be sitting on a woven rattan chair in a Bandung living room surrounded by Scrabble tiles. At 3:19 p.m. that day, Zack and I were supposed to be splashing in the waves of the Indian Ocean.

○ ○ ○

Survivors later described the sound of the incoming tsunami as something like a low-flying airplane. People covered their ears, scanning the clouds for the source of the noise, more curious than afraid. The force of the coming wave had sucked back the shoreline, exposing bare wet sand as the shallows fled to join a swelling wall of water.

At its highest point, the wave reached over twenty meters, roughly as tall as a seven-story building. According to one police report, 668 people were killed by the impact or swept away to drown at sea. Houses and shopfronts nearest the beach were reduced to rubble, crushing their inhabitants. Chunks of wood and concrete torn away by the rushing water became weapons farther inland.

In the alternate universe where Zack never got sick, that death toll rises from 668 to 670. Zack's dad might have been back at the hotel, shielded by its sturdy concrete walls from the worst of the impact. (Though I should clarify, lest you think sturdy concrete walls solve tsunamis, that the entire first floor of our usual hotel was destroyed, and a car ended up in the swimming pool.) Zack's dad might have survived.

But the prospects for Zack and me are less optimistic.

The scene plays out the same way in my head every time. The distant offshore earthquake, so faint we don't even feel it amid the crashing waves. The ominous receding shoreline, noticed too late. The frantic shouts of fellow swimmers, fingers outstretched toward the mammoth wave forming on the horizon. Swimming like we've never swum before, racing inland, buoyed forward and then pulled backward by the current. When the tsunami catches us, we turn invisible inside it, tumbling through sand and salt foam, losing all sense of up and down, tossed about like jetsam.

There are plenty of people to whom this story belongs much more than it belongs to me. There are eyewitness accounts of the Pangandaran tsunami from survivors whose brush with death was immediate and palpable. I was two hundred kilometers away at the time, nowhere close to danger, strategizing how to get double points for my x's and q's. And yet, the alternate universe where Zack never got sick—the universe I once wanted so badly—has always felt only a hairsbreadth away from reality.

"Weren't you supposed to be in Pangandaran today?" someone asked as we sat around the living room table in Bandung, intermittently praying and scouring the internet for news updates, our Scrabble tiles forgotten.

"Yes," I said, the weight of the answer just beginning to strike me.

"Just think," they said, "if Zack hadn't gotten sick . . ."

No one finished the sentence.

○ ○ ○

When I was in middle school, I read a novel called *Castaways of the Flying Dutchman*. Let me spoil the premise for you: a young boy and a dog on a ship in the Atlantic Ocean are washed overboard during a storm. Just as they're about to die, an angel appears, rescuing them and making them immortal. From then on, the duo travels the world helping people. Since they don't age, they can never stay in one place for too long, lest their secret immortality be discovered. Every few months or years, they are forced to disappear again, find a new person or community in need of their help, and establish a new sense of belonging. There can be no marriage, no family, no settling down. They never get a normal life. Instead, they are given something far grander—and far more excruciating.

I recall, perhaps foolishly, feeling some jealousy for those two castaways and their ghostly angelic existence. It wasn't the living forever that appealed to me particularly—I was already anticipating heavenly immortality for myself. What I craved, rather, was their clarity of purpose. Because they had been as good as dead, every bit of life they lived after their rescue was owed to someone else, to some calling larger than themselves. They didn't belong to any one place in the world, because they didn't belong to themselves at all. And yet, because they knew their purpose, they knew precisely where they were meant to be.

We live differently, I think, when we come to see ourselves as people whose lives have stopped belonging to us.

It's one thing to say abstractly that you've been spared from death. It's quite another thing to feel it concretely, to watch news footage of the devastation you accidentally missed, to visit the scene months later and still see piles of rubble and walls stained with water damage. When I looked out at the Pangandaran waterline, I saw the death I should have had, my waterlogged body floating at sea, eyes open but unseeing. I felt myself peel away from my own corpse like a ghost, like an immortalized boy or an anthropomorphic dog rescued out of the ocean and set on a divine mission.

In that moment of terrifying clarity, I told God that I wanted to live like I wasn't owed anything anymore. I wanted my moments to belong to a purpose that exceeded me. I wanted to live like one of the castaways.

I wanted to live as if I had already died.

It would have been nice if this ghostly angelic rebirth of mine had come with a new gossamer body. Maybe my change of heart would have stuck a bit better if I could have seen it in the mirror. As it was, I still looked and felt so ordinary. More often than not, I still acted in ordinary ways. But every once in a while, when I found myself getting angry at God for depriving me of some happiness I believed I deserved, I would flash back to the scene of my death, and I would remember that I had already relinquished the right to live a life ordered toward my own happiness. It's harder to be angry with God when you stop believing God owes you something.

Maybe this is why our new life in Christ is marked by baptism. Because if we want to truly live, we first need to face our death. We need to feel it, to sink beneath the waves in symbolic burial. Our old dreams and expectations and demands need to slip from our fingers and drift down to a watery grave. We need to emerge empty-handed, grasping nothing, dripping grace.

"You died," the apostle Paul tells a bunch of still-very-much-biologically-alive people in Colossians 3, "and your life is now hidden with Christ in God." The fact of our Christian death matters supremely—not because we remain dead, but because life-before-death and life-after-death are fundamentally at odds with each other. Our new life is no longer ours at all. It is *hidden*: placed outside of us, beyond our control, insulated from every attempt to enhance or diminish it. There's nothing we can do to add to it anymore, no sense chasing the "good life" for ourselves. And there's nothing left to fear, either, because the hidden life can't be taken away from us. Death has no power to kill a resurrected ghost.

Living like the already dead is not the exception of Christian life, reserved for the occasional castaway or tsunami survivor. Death is the rule, the norm, the sine qua non. Or it ought to be.

One of the great dangers of twenty-first-century Western evangelical Christianity, I fear, is that too many of us have grown accustomed to resurrection without death. Our faith has room for empty crosses but not for occupied ones. We quote Jeremiah 29:11 out of context, not by accident but quite on purpose, because we prefer the idea of a religion in which all God's plans are made for *us*, to prosper *us*, to shield *us* from harm, to give *us* a hope and a future. We decide in advance what constitutes a good life and then hire God on as a divine contractor (at a negotiable hourly rate) to help *us* achieve *our* goals. We call them God's plans, yes, but they are ours in their inception and direction, and his only in the sense that we have attributed them to him.

I know people who are so sure God will bless them with a spouse and two-and-a-quarter well-groomed children in perfect physical and mental health. So sure God has the perfect job lined up for them, neither too challenging nor too boring, complete with dental benefits and a nice retirement package. So sure God wants to prosper their nation, protect their family, polish their reputation, preserve their friendships, stock their pantry, and help them find their lost car keys.

It's possible that God does indeed desire to give all these things, at least to some of us, some of the time. But if these are our aims, our religion is merely a self-centered enterprise, a means to the same good life we would have been chasing anyway.

If we don't want the Jesus who might call us to celibacy or childlessness or heartbreak or ignominy, we don't want Jesus. If we don't want the Jesus who might eject us from a perfect job and an idyllic neighborhood so we can serve an unfamiliar community and die young of a mysterious tropical illness, we don't want Jesus. If we don't want the Jesus whose standard of love and hospitality and generosity toward those in need is so impractical and profligate that it might leave us mistreated and penniless, we don't want Jesus.

Jesus wants to bless us, yes. But he wants to bless us the upside-down way, with the kind of blessing that counterintuitively emerges by way of utter ruination. We find our lives only after first losing them, and not a moment sooner. There are no shortcuts to Christian death, as Johanna Finegan so rightly said in her keynote address at the 2019 Revoice conference: "You can't tell God, *Hey, since you're gonna be giving me my life back anyway, how about I just hang onto it and we'll call it even?*"

If all we want from Jesus is the glittering accessories of resurrection, with none of that pesky death along the way, we might have confused Jesus with Walmart.

We can't emerge from the water of baptism until we are first willing to sink beneath it. Jesus doesn't offer resurrection without death. Death is resurrection's only point of entry.

○ ○ ○

According to some accounts, when a Roman general in the early centuries CE paraded through a city to celebrate his military triumphs, a servant would follow a few steps behind him repeating (among other things) the Latin phrase *memento mori*: "Remember that you will die." The practice was meant to keep the general humble, to confront him with his humanity, to remind him that no amount of victory could obviate his eventual demise.

Memento mori. Remember that you will die. Remember that you are dust, and to dust you will return.

This was the first of the realities that struck me when the tsunami came. I am mortal. Not just mortal in a categorical, textbook kind of way, once I reach the statistically ripe old age of seventy-nine. Not just *eventually* mortal. I am mortal in this moment—striding or sprinting or lollygagging toward the hour of my death. It's never farther away than a smudge on the CT scan, a patch of ice beneath the tire, a seemingly random change of plans.

Life on earth belongs to us the way a leaf belongs to a branch: sometimes plucked or cut off, sometimes carried away by the breeze, sometimes clinging tightly until winter claims it. But never permanent. Never ours to keep.

Memento mori.

One of the joys of studying Latin is that, if you ignore English sentence structure and just woodenly substitute words for each other, you can wind up with some entertaining translations. Here, compliments of eight weeks of summer intensive Latin in grad school, is my literal translation of *memento mori*: "Remember to die."

When I first rendered this translation, I found it hilarious. ("Don't forget to buy milk on the way home, and pick up the dry cleaning. Oh, and also, remember to die.") But the longer I sit with it, the more I meditate on my sloppy Latin, the more I believe Jesus' followers need this reminder too. Or at least, I do.

Memento mori, Greg. Remember to die.

Remember that the call to follow Jesus is nothing more or less than a call to let go of everything you thought you needed. Don't let your enthusiasm for resurrection cause you to bypass the grave.

Remember that you should have died in a tsunami. And because you're still here, live a life that belongs to something bigger than you.

21

Rivers Cannot
Sweep It Away

Notes from an Alien Anthropologist:
Despite their highly developed brains, the human creatures suffer from faulty memories. They feel the need to schedule regular reminders of their romance, their country's existence, even their own birth. Their most life-altering truths require constant repetition.

I'm not the sort of guy you'd expect to have a tattoo. Tattoos are for guys who moonlight as avant-garde artists. For sailors and military men. For CrossFitters, trendy pastors with shaved heads, hipsters who use organic beard oil, and guys who unironically call each other "bro." Or so the stereotype goes.

By now, you probably know me well enough to know that I am none of these guys.

You might be wondering, then, how I ended up on a table in a tattoo parlor with my left sleeve rolled up to the shoulder. You might be wondering why my jaw and fist are clenched, why Carrie the TCK is standing nearby telling outlandish stories to distract me, why a tattoo artist named Gab is wielding a little whirring machine that keeps stabbing me with a needle as if my bicep is a quilt being sewn together.

Frankly, I'm wondering the same thing. (And so is Gab the tattoo artist, probably. But she says nothing. She's a professional.)

○ ○ ○

Like many Christian youths, I sang the hymn "Come Thou Fount" long before I knew what it meant to "raise my Ebenezer." The only Ebenezer I knew at the time was Ebenezer Scrooge. I pictured myself raising a miserly old man above my head, as if he was Simba and I was Rafiki in the opening scene of *The Lion King*.

It wasn't until college that I heard the Ebenezer explained in such a way that I remembered it. The reference comes from 1 Samuel 7, where the Israelites are filled with fear because of an approaching Philistine army. They cry out to God, who intervenes with a massive thunderstorm that sends the Philistines into a panicked retreat. The prophet Samuel commemorates the victory by setting up a stone he names *Ebenezer*, Hebrew for "stone of help." "Thus far," says Samuel, "the LORD has helped us." (Here's a fun language tip: the Hebrew word for "help," *ezer*, is the same word that appears in Genesis 2 when God decides to make Eve as a "helper" for Adam. Next time someone tells you that Eve's "helper" status makes her subordinate to Adam, ask them if God's "helper" status makes him subordinate to Israel.)

You might not think the Israelites would have a problem remembering God's miraculous help. But God seems to expect them to act like spiritual amnesiacs.

And sure enough, they do.

In 1 Samuel 8, one chapter after their spectacular salvation from the Philistines, the Israelites reject the idea of God's kingship over them and ask Samuel to appoint a human king instead. Likewise, in Exodus 14, two chapters after their miraculous departure from Egypt, the Israelites are doubting God's faithfulness and wishing to return to slavery. This cycle repeats itself throughout the whole Old Testament: God's people are in trouble, they cry out to him, he saves the day, they forget about him, and trouble overtakes them again.

My friend J-Marks and I got to talking about these vexing Israelite tendencies during dinner at Panera one evening while I was in grad school. "I want to feel morally superior to the Israelites," I told J-Marks between bites of panini. "They seem so stupid and forgetful. God blows their minds with his faithfulness in one verse, and then they start doubting him again six verses later. But I think my memory is even worse than the Israelites' memories. They sometimes go for an entire generation before they start drifting away from God. I can barely last two weeks without doubting all the ways God has already proven himself to me."

"Maybe that's why the Israelites kept building memorials," said J-Marks. "As a way of trying to make their memories last longer."

I buttered half a baguette as I pondered the point. "But I'm not sure rock piles work as well in twenty-first-century America as they did in ancient Israel. I could stack a couple boulders in the front lawn of my apartment complex, but I don't think they'd stick around for long. Land doesn't have the kind of permanence it used to have. What are we modern folks supposed to do if we want to remember something forever?"

"There are tattoos . . ." said J-Marks.

"I'm not the sort of guy who would ever get a tattoo," I told him. "But if I did get a tattoo, that would probably be my reason."

○ ○ ○

I've never doubted the faithfulness of God more than I did in the months between deciding to come out as a celibate gay Christian and actually coming out. Once I'd signed the book contract, I knew there was no going back. But that knowledge didn't keep me from feeling irrationally afraid of everything that might change.

Of everything that might be lost.

When I looked back at all the ways God had worked to bring me to the present moment, I could begrudgingly say with the prophet Samuel, "Thus far the Lord has helped me." But in those months of anticipation, my life felt like God's fingerprints were coated with dust, like grace was a bottle about to run out, already drained to its final drops. I tried to imagine the future, and all I saw was ominous, inscrutable darkness.

I would lie in bed for hours after waking up, no longer tired but wishing to still be asleep. Wishing I could never have to wake up again.

And still the world kept moving rudely onward, despite my misgivings. I still had a PhD dissertation to write. My publisher was still prepping me for authorship, eagerly awaiting the moment when life as I knew it might end. I had a list of over one hundred people to come out to, whether in person or by email, before I took the plunge and posted the news on Facebook; I hacked away at my list bit by bit, a few emails a night. The children's director at my church wanted to know if I could help with the music at our sports camp that summer, and I was waiting to answer him until I knew how much of a crisis my coming out would cause for our congregation.

Eleven days before coming out, on the loneliest night of my life (so far), I sent my pastor an email at exactly 1:00 a.m.:

Dear Aaron,

It's late, and I can't turn my brain off. *Maybe if I write something*, I tell myself. But writing feels so solipsistic sometimes. It's not just that I want to turn things into words: it's that I want to be heard, to be heard by someone more than just me and Jesus. (Not that Jesus isn't good company.) Anyway, that means I need to write to someone, and I picked you. (Thanks for being such an obvious choice.) (Sorry this means you'll be subjected to my post-midnight ramblings.)

When I got home tonight, I'd gotten emails from both my parents confirming that, as far as they were concerned, I could share the news of my book publicly whenever I wanted to.

So I wrote them back a nice little newsy email, full of exclamation points and smiley faces, because that's just how I roll. Everything is grand. (Isn't it?)

Then I tried to write an email to Bill Jester, asking him if I could have a little more time to think about Sports Camp because, um, my summer might be, well, when did he need a final answer by, maybe I could, um . . .

I didn't finish that email. But I'll be damned if the draft didn't have exclamation points and smiley faces in it. (Pardon the PG-13 language. Don't read this email aloud to your children.)

I ate a bowl of cereal and washed a few dishes. When I ran out of dishes to wash, I stayed hunched over the sink, water still running, staring at my hands. I'm not quite sure how long I stood there before I realized I was crying. (Why bother turning off one faucet when you can't turn the other one off?)

I can't do this, I whispered to myself—or perhaps to God, if we want to give me a little credit—over and over again.

Here's the trouble with angsty Greg: his pronouns have no antecedents. What is the "this" I can't do? Is it the coming out? The waiting-poised-to-come-out-but-not-quite-there-yet-and-dreading-it-and-wishing-it-could-be-over-all-at-once? The being an author? The anticipation of whatever accolades or condemnations might accompany it? The fear of never again being able to lead worship without wondering if people are distracted because I'm gay? The knowing that people could read about my life—my life—and use it as a talking point, like tomorrow's weather forecast or the fine markings on a Grecian urn?

Hard to say. They all feel pretty tangled up right now. But whatever "this" is, my heart remains convinced that I can't do it. Unfortunately, it seems my head has failed to properly alert my heart that I'm already doing it, or at least that I'm well past the point of no return.

You said a few months ago that I might need to give myself permission to be human. It worked—I'm feeling very human. (Remind me again how humans go on breathing?)

There's so much in my life that's glorious. (Really, tons of things. I lead a delightful life.) And these particular sorrows are part of the glory, when I think about it. So I don't mean to sound whiny or ungrateful. I'm just trying to admit how thoroughly small and confused and human I feel. I'm just a guy who lies on his bed staring at the ceiling, with tears trickling out the corner of one eye, wishing it could all be over now, because my imagination is unbearably prolific in the meantime.

I can't do this. Not tonight.

But maybe I can fall asleep. And if I wake up, maybe I'll be able to do it tomorrow.

Love always (because I'm sure of at least that much, when I'm sure of nothing else),

Greg

I did indeed fall asleep. I woke up the next day, too. (Which was, statistically speaking, the most probable outcome.) And the world was bearable again. Or almost bearable. Or still unbearable, but in such a way that it didn't seem to matter so much whether I was capable of bearing it.

In his email back to me, Aaron wrote, "I'm pretty sure that every hero of the faith . . . has had SIGNIFICANT times or seasons of saying, 'I can't do it.' The interesting thing is that we usually read their story with some perspective of how it ends, a perspective that the hero did not have in the moments that felt like despair."

He listed a bunch of examples of heroic faith—from Bible characters like Moses and Joshua and Peter to recent icons like Harriet Tubman and Teresa of Calcutta—who had felt insufficient to bear the weight of their calling. At the end of the list of heroes, he facetiously added his own name. "It's my email," he wrote, "so I can lump myself in with whomever I want."

As I think back on my own season of feeling unable to continue, it seems oddly beautiful. I see, with the wisdom of three years' retrospect, the ways God was poised to show off his faithfulness, the ways he always continued to be faithful even in moments that felt like despair. *Coles*, I want to tell three-year-younger me, *pull yourself together. You've already known so much of the love of God. You should have collected enough data by now to trust that his love isn't going anywhere.*

But reproachful present-day Coles will probably turn out to be a hypocrite. Even now, with all the new data I've gathered, I'm still not immune to doubt, not immune to feeling that God has withdrawn and become absent. I have a hunch that I'll discover, in some future season of even greater challenge, that my memory is still as short as ever.

Grace is a funny thing. It should have all the predictability of a romantic comedy, and yet I always find myself watching it as if it's a thriller, on the edge of my seat, not quite sure how everything will turn out.

○ ○ ○

"I've been thinking about marriage symbols," I told my author friend Deb as we sat in a crowded hotel lobby. "When people get married, they make promises to each other. They throw a party so all their friends know about the promises. They exchange rings as a physical symbol of their promises. They consummate the promises with their bodies. But when I promise myself to God in celibate singleness, I don't do any of that. I just keep on muddling along in my singleness."

"Well, maybe you *should* do something," said Deb in her flawless Australian accent, waving a hand over her wine glass. "Maybe you need something to remember your promises by, some symbolic consummation of your celibacy."

"Like a celibate wedding ring?" I said.

"Why not?" she said. "Or anything. Anything you can hold onto even in the moments when you don't want to hold onto anything."

A month later, in a cabin in the woods of central Pennsylvania, I asked my married friend Cooper what he'd think if I tattooed a wedding ring onto my finger. A taxidermied moose head watched us from the far wall as Cooper rocked in his chair and pondered the idea. "I like it," he said at last, pointing a hand toward me. "But if I were in your shoes, I wouldn't settle for a ring. I'd want to tweak the symbol a bit, get creative with it, make it specific to you and Jesus. After all, your relationship with Jesus is much deeper and broader than a human marriage. Why sell it short? Why borrow someone else's symbol when your own promises have a unique kind of beauty?"

○ ○ ○

I found my tattoo while I was reading chapter 8 of the Song of Solomon in the Septuagint: ὕδωρ πολὺ οὐ δυνήσεται σβέσαι τὴν ἀγάπην, καὶ ποταμοὶ οὐ συγκλύσουσιν αὐτήν. *Many waters cannot quench love, and rivers cannot sweep it away.* The Greek letters encircle my left arm in a ring, like a wedding band pulled up over my bicep. Each time the sentence ends, it begins again, its poetry never completed, continuing on forever.

Forever, like promises.

Forever, like love.

Above the whir of the tattoo machine, I think the words loudly, as if I'm reciting a wedding vow to a tender divine Lover. I think the words until they become more captivating than the story Carrie is telling. Until their promise feels tighter than my clenched fist. Until they're sharper and bolder and more indelible than the lines Gab the tattoo artist is carving into my skin:

Many waters cannot quench love.

The words are reciprocal, running from heaven to me and back again, a promise made both *by* me and *to* me. When the tsunami comes to claim me, I'm not letting go, and neither is he.

Rivers cannot sweep it away.

I am my Beloved's. He is mine. We belong in one another, with one another, to one another. We always will. We're not going anywhere.

I'm not the only one making these vows with heaven, to be sure. A symphony of voices joins mine in the air. The song includes married folks as well as celibates like me, straight and gay and everything else. Our choir represents every race, every language, every nation.

But despite the grandeur of the choir, Christ still hears and responds to each individual voice. He isn't content to declare his affection for us in form letters and megaphone announcements. He whispers to us one by one, into your ear and mine, exchanging promises of love. As long as these promises remain true—as long as our fragile memories can hold them—home will never be further than a whisper in our ears, never further than an ink drop beneath our skin.

We are loved. And because we are loved, we belong.

Shore

Broken seashells and bottle caps buried in sand
Hardly a manuscript page fit for an author's hand
But you scrawled your love upon my shore
And I finally began to understand what I was made for

At midnight the moon pulled the tide like a blanket up to her chin
Rinsing away all the evidence of where you'd been
When the tide fell back, the shore was bare
And I started to wonder if you'd ever really been there

Forgetful
I'm so forgetful

But you, sure as the day
Love with a love that can't be washed away
And I beg you to make my memories strong
So I never forget you even when you feel gone

The scavengers combed me for treasure but left empty-handed
If alone is the same thing as lonely, I'm already stranded
But you caught the wave back to my shore
And traced into the sand again the things that I was made for

Maybe I'll keep on forgetting as tides keep on rising
But maybe, if I keep on begging, you will keep writing

Acknowledgments

If you're hunting for your name in these acknowledgments, it should probably be in here. But alas, word limits. Just as this book isn't nearly long enough to fit all the stories of countless dear friends with whom I belong, so the thanks I owe far exceed my available ink.

Still, in the words of Lin-Manuel Miranda's Hamilton, "I'm not throwing away my shot."

Mike Nappa: Your agenting and mentoring have transformed my writing life. My heart sinks every time you tell me "there's still work to be done before it's ready to show to publishers," and this project was no exception. But as usual, the outcome was so worth the perspiration.

Ethan McCarthy: I hope you've had half as much fun editing me as I've had being edited by you. I can't think of anyone better suited to guide and shape this manuscript from infancy to (relative) maturity. You're no gubbins.

The whole InterVarsity Press team: Working with you has been sheer delight. From that first brainstorming call with Cindy Bunch, to the passionate marketing advocacy of Lori Neff and Krista Clayton, to David Fassett's exquisite cover design, to Lisa Rieck's assiduous copyediting, to the support of Ellen Hsu and Rebecca Gill and Kathryn Chapek and Maila Kue on dozens of details great and small, and so much more from so many others—thank you for bringing this book to life with me.

Julia Sadusky, Rachel Gilson, Laurie Krieg, and Curry Kennedy: Thanks for hashing out key ideas with me, reading over drafted bits, and helping me sound smarter than I have any right to sound.

Carrie and Evan Gingrich: I know I hogged the kitchen table while I was drafting this manuscript. Forgive me for continuing to hog it now that the book is finished.

Rachel Fawcett: Approximately one-third of my revision process consisted of you prodding me awake every time I fell asleep at the computer. Some of my finest sentences owe you their lives.

Zack and Anna Filbert: You're both permanently hired as my design consultants. (And everything else too. Got Thanksgiving plans?)

Nathanael Filbert: I'm rarely called photogenic, but somehow you've worked magic. Your expertise is rivaled only by your generosity and friendship.

Mom, Dad, and beloved siblings in- and out-of-law: If I gushed nearly as much as I ought to about how wonderful you are, everyone would be rightfully jealous. Take this paralipsis as a token of my boundless affection.

The four dozen people who consented to be named in this book: Thanks for letting me immortalize you in print. What an impoverished life I would have led if our stories had never overlapped.

The motley, beautiful community of LGBTQ and same-sex-attracted people seeking to follow Jesus: Thank you for inspiring this book and for reminding me that the best company in the world is found among those radically committed to the gospel. In the words of my twin, Tyler Chernesky, "You will never regret any decision you make to become more like Jesus."

And you, dear reader: Thank you for sharing these pages with me. I pray that you would find Jesus within them, and that he would prove himself even more lovely in your life than he has proven himself in mine.